Adolescent
Separation Anxiety
VOLUME II

Adolescent Separation Anxiety
VOLUME II

SEPARATION DISORDERS

by
Henry G. Hansburg

A Manual for the Clinical Interpretation of The Separation Anxiety Test

ROBERT E. KRIEGER PUBLISHING COMPANY
HUNTINGTON, NEW YORK
1980

Original edition 1980

Printed and Published by
ROBERT E. KRIEGER PUBLISHING CO., INC.
645 NEW YORK AVENUE
HUNTINGTON, NEW YORK 11743

Copyright © 1980 by
ROBERT E. KRIEGER PUBLISHING CO., INC.

Printed in the United States of America

Library of Congress Cataloging in Publication Data (Revised)
Hansburg, Henry G.   1910–
  Adolescent separation anxiety.

  Vol. 1 was first published in 1972 under title: Adolescent separation anxiety; a method for the study of adolescent separation problems.
  Bibliography: p.
  Includes index.
  CONTENTS: v. 1. A method for the study of adolescent separation problems. – v. 2. Separation disorders.
  1. Separation anxiety in children. 2. Separation (Psychology) 3. Adolescent psychology. I. Title.
BF724.S38H35   1979   616.8'522   79-21798
ISBN 0-89874-042-8 (v. 2)
     0-89874-043-6 (v. 2)

Acknowledgments

I wish to thank the psychological staff of the psychiatric clinic of the Jewish Child Care Association of New York City for their interest and cooperation in working with the Separation Anxiety Test during the four-year period subsequent to the publication of Volume I. I am especially indebted to Miss Christine Duplak and Dr. Martin Vigdor, psychologists, for their continuing and uninterrupted support during that time. I am also grateful to Dr. Vigdor for his assistance in editing the second draft of this manuscript, which formed a good basis for the present third draft.

Further, my sincere thanks go to Dr. Allen Blumstein, of the Court Referral Project of Kings County Hospital (New York City), to Dr. Nucia Shimrat, the psychiatric clinic of Mt. Sinai Hospital (New York City), and to Dr. George Sackheim, supervisor of psychological services at the Pleasantville (New Jersey) Cottage School and of the diagnostic center, all of whom were instrumental in the administration of the Separation Anxiety Test at their centers. My thanks go to Mr. David Roth for his executive permission to carry on the technical problems of putting together the material of this book and to the administrative staff of the psychiatric clinic of the Jewish Child Care Association under the direction of Dr. Sol Nichtern, chief psychiatrist, for permission to present many papers on the use of the test at staff meetings.

I should also like to express my indebtedness to the staff members of the California School for Professional Psychology in Los Angeles, especially Dr. Karl Pottharst and one of his students, Dr. Pauline DeLozier, for their interest in the use of the test in research studies and for the frequent seminars I have been privileged to provide for doctoral candidates at the school. Finally, I am deeply grateful to Dr. John Bowlby, of the Tavistock Institute in London, for his continued active interest in my work and for his efforts to enlist the participation of the psychiatric and psychological professions in the use of the instrument.

H.G.H.

To my dear wife, Rose,
who for nearly half a century has been
my most cherished companion
and affectionate caretaker

PREFACE

This book is the second volume dealing with the use of the Separation Anxiety Test in the clinical evaluation of separated children and adolescents. The first volume, Adolescent Separation Anxiety: A Method for the Study of Adolescent Separation Problems, was published by Charles C. Thomas in 1972 and recently reprinted by Robert E. Krieger Publishing Company (1980). In Volume I the original experiments in the development of the Separation Anxiety Test are described and the principal clinical concepts of the test are explained.

Since the publication of Volume I much progress has been made in the use and interpretation of studies of separation problems both in clinical work and in research. Moreover, we are now much more aware of theoretical implications of the clinical findings through the extension of attachment theory to the method, as developed by John Bowlby. Hence the title of this volume, *Separation Disorders*, in which we attempt to delineate these disorders and to relate them to significant psychological systems. In so doing we have found it possible to describe individual psychological separation problems from the protocols of the Separation Anxiety Test with greater and more accurately incisive detail.

Since the original publication of Volume I, the method was revised by Bowlby and Klagsbrun (1976) for use with young children. The method has also been applied to adults by DeLozier (1979), to whole families by Hansburg (see p. 144 of this volume), and to the elderly by Hansburg (in press). Many studies are now being conducted at the California School of Professional Psychology in which this method is used in cases of divorced parents, children of separated parents, and other related cases. This method is also employed in studies of delinquents at the Youth Development Center in New Castle, Pennsylvania; and in a study of college freshmen living away from their parents at the Counseling Center of Michigan State University. Volume III of this series will provide a discussion of these studies.

Fourteen years ago I began the work of developing an objective method for the study of separation problems, which I refer to as *Separation Disorders,* the title of this volume. My search for answers along theoretical as well as clinical lines has led me to incorporate the concepts and findings of Bowlby, Mahler, Ainsworth, Winnicott, Freud, Harlow, White, and others. I have been trying to understand the numerous ramifications of emotional reactions, intrapsychic movements, behavior and personality traits in human beings during daily separation experiences and during unusual or traumatic experiences. A full understanding of disturbances precipitated by separations is often elusive, because each new enlightenment is followed by new questions, which continue to plague us. Yet despite these new questions, I have been able to delineate to some degree various types of emotional and behavioral disorders which I have considered referrable to the developmental separation process and to the manner in which youngsters have reacted to this process within their particular families and community milieu.

I have been mindful that the development of adequate attachments and of the ability to deal with separations are not the only sources of emotional growth. Nor do all pathological conditions arise out of failures in the separation-individuation process (Mahler and Masterson notwithstanding). Biological handicaps, ego malfunctions, nonseparating traumatic events, and other factors, play significant roles not only in object relations but also in pathological disorders. Yet the discoveries of the preceding three or four decades relating to the instinctive need for protection manifested in primate (Harlow, 1970) and human (Bowlby, 1969, and

Ainsworth, 1979) attachments have opened up avenues of investigation highly significant in the study of pathology.

Bowlby has described several types of disorder he considers to be associated with disruption of affectional bonds (attachment)—psychopathic or sociopathic personality, suicidal persons, and depressives. He states: "It is proving productive to view many of the psychoneurotic and personality disturbances of humans as being reflections of a disturbed capacity for making affectional bonds, due either to faulty development during childhood or to subsequent derangement." (1969)

Studying the opposite side of behavior, referred to as "self-reliance" (1973) Bowlby states: ". . . these well-adapted personalities show a smoothly working balance of, on the one hand, initiative and self-reliance, and, on the other, a capacity both to seek help and to make use of help when occasion demands. . . . Evidence presented suggests that both self-reliance and the capacity to rely on others are alike products of a family that provides strong support for its offspring combined with respect for their personal aspirations, their sense of responsibility, and their ability to deal with the world."

It is the recognition of this balance as the interdependence between these two factors that forms the theoretical bedrock for the interpretation of personality disorders obtained from the Separation Anxiety Test. The validity of this technique has been largely verified by clinical experience and has been of considerable aid in understanding dynamic reactions referred to as "separation disorders." Using pictures of separation situations of both mild and strong import has provided us with rich clinical material as well as apparent verification of the concepts of attachment theory. It is my firm hope that this method will come into wider use in clinical settings as well as in research because of its capacity to detect disorders related to separation experiences.

New York City, 1980   Henry G. Hansburg

TABLE OF CONTENTS

CHAPTER

I

PSYCHOLOGICAL SYSTEMS
AND SEPARATION DISORDERS

So far as is known, the term *separation disorders* has not as yet found its way into the literature on attachment and separation. The reason seems primarily related to diagnostic terminology commonly used in psychiatry and psychology with regard to personality and emotional disturbances, such as anxiety neurosis, hysteria, character disorder, and the like. Thus, for most mental health professionals disturbances resulting from separation from significant persons, places, or things are considered to be largely consequences of more fundamental disorders. They have been attributed to developmental and internal dynamic forces unrelated to attachment which go awry. These forces are largely sexual and/or aggressive in nature.

With the appearance of the works by Bowlby (1969, 1973) on attachment and separation, it has become clearer that the need for attachment is so fundamental for survival that unless this need is adequately gratified and developed, the potential for personality and behavioral disturbance is considerable. It follows from attachment theory that threats of such separation or actual separation from significant attachment figures produces varying degrees of emotional and behavioral distress. The nature of the resultant disturbance depends upon what has occurred before the disturbance and what patterns of response have been established. It seems reasonable to refer to such patterns of response as separation disorders.

Therefore, a *separation disorder* can be conceived as a pattern of dysfunctioning or pathological psychological systems aroused inappropriately by separation experiences. These dysfunctional psychological systems are set in motion whenever any separation is experienced either in retrospect because of some current stress, because of some present shifts in environmental conditions (vocation, home, and others), because of a recent loss of an attachment figure, or because of the prospect of an impending abandonment or dislocation.

The term *psychological system* is represented by both cognitive and affective unconscious patterned reactions developed over many years by constant repetitive processing (Bowlby, 1980). On a conscious level the psychological system is translated into a behavioral system. When the system becomes dysfunctional, inappropriate, or pathological in the presence of separation threats or experiences and affects other systems, this condition is referred to as a separation disorder.

A psychological system seems to be similar to a physiological system—for example, respiratory, digestive, circulatory, glandular. Although each function is autonomous to some degree and plays a very specific role in the economy of the organism, it is fully integrated with the other systems; and when it is dysfunctioning, it may have a very definite disrupting effect on the other systems. Each psychological system represents well-known psychological constructs having both unconscious dynamics and behavioral consequences. While each has an autonomous function to some degree, it is in constant interaction with the other psychological systems and disturbances in one affect the condition of the others—sometimes mildly and temporarily and occasionally seriously and long term.

Since many psychological systems have from time to time made their way into various formulations of a theoretical nature, no attempt is made here to explore all the possibilities. In the context of this study of separation, those which relate most specifically to this area of human experience are considered. Neither is an effort made to suggest the normal or typical reactions of these psychological systems, because the emphasis is on pathology (although from time to time references are made to normative patterns for comparative purposes).

The Attachment System

The primary psychological system aroused by the concern over separation is attachment. This system has been described to some extent in a previous volume (Hansburg, 1972). The best delineation of the system has been provided by Bowlby (1969) and more recently, in infancy, by Ainsworth (1979) and does not require any extensive elaboration here. The system may be defined as a propensity for mammals, especially primates and anthropoids, to seek proximity to another for the instinctual purpose of protection and subsequently for other elaborated and sophisticated gratifications geared to survival. The system is characterized by intrapsychic reactions (sensory, perceptive, cognitive, and affective) as well as by behaviors designed to obtain or induce proximity.

There has been a good deal of discussion and controversy about attachment and dependency and about the degree to which they are related and essentially different. Bowlby has been negatively critical of the term dependency as it has been used in psychoanalysis and in its literature. He considers dependency as a generally pejorative term that has been confused with attachment. The difference between these two concepts is studied quite thoroughly in an edited work by Gewirtz (1972) in which contributions were made by Ainsworth and others. The term dependency needs is constantly referred to in psychoanalysis as a characterization of the need to be dependent upon an attachment figure, and the recognition of this inner need is thought essential to health. In this sense the term is very similar to Bowlby's concept of attachment.

Although attachment is usually referred to as a behavioral system, the evidence appears to suggest that it represents a highly organized unconscious as well as conscious patterning. The system is not purely a construct nor is it reserved only for a particular individual, as suggested by Ainsworth (1972). Once organized and developed through various experiences, the system is readily elicited by another individual, place, or object that has characteristics similar to other significant attachment figures during the pattern's formation.

Since the propensity for proximity-seeking, especially with an attachment figure, is based on organismic trends built in as a survival measure, it seems likely that humans vary from individual to individual in the intensity and extent of this trend. The evidence for variability in all human characteristics from birth has been demonstrated in many studies (Thomas, Chess, and Birch, 1968; Fries and Woolf, 1953). Although these variations may be attributed to the ups and downs of caretaking behavior, the evidence from developmental studies of children in the same families suggests that the mother's behavioral interaction with her children is to some degree traceable to the infant's own developmental idiosyncratic behavior. It seems likely that we are dealing with a complicated interaction variability in the extent of attachment propensity and at the same time variability in the caretaker's reactions to the particular variations in the children.

Whereas life experience with the unfolding of the attachment system is based upon this early patterning, there is increasing indication that intense new experiences as well as traumatic events can alter the nature of this system. In this respect, opinion differs vastly, even among psychoanalysts. This difference was given its greatest impetus in 1960 when Bowlby's attachment theory received wide publicity. If this thesis is not correct, the fundamental basis for psychoanalytic efforts to alter the nature of the system in any given individual would have to be abandoned. What is stated here is that although the attachment system, once firmly established, exercises considerable power over behavior, it still remains viable to some degree. (Kagan, 1978; Bowlby, 1960)

The Individuation (Self-Reliance) System

Movement away from an attachment figure requires a degree of individuation (Mahler, 1968) or self-reliance (Bowlby, 1973). This system of both intrapsychic and behavioral content requires a degree of integration of the forces within the organism—the propensity to explore and utilize the environment for the gratification of many other systems. This has been referred to by Ainsworth (1972) as exploratory behavior and by Witkin (1962) as psychological differentiation. The more the individual is propelled by the top of the hierarchy, the self-system (ego), the more he moves away from the attachment figure and the more he manifests exploratory behavior. At the same time the evidence suggests that without the availablity or accessibility of the attachment figure, the functioning of the system of self-reliance is limited.

This psychological system represents a long-term patterning development. The degree to which it is readily disrupted and blocked is highly related to what has been and is occurring within the attachment system. Threats of separation from meaningful persons, places, or objects tend to reduce the functioning of this system and conversely to increase the activity of the attachment system. Further, unsuccessful exploratory behavior because of lack of skill, competence, or effectance may also increase the activity of the attachment system (White, 1963).

Continued disruption of this system produces a variety of disorders, some including intense efforts at self-sufficiency—a narcissitic dependence on self—and others indicating varying degrees of helplessness related to locating attachment figures for sustenance and for action in the person's behalf. Separation experiences or threats of abandonment are known to produce such disruptions. Experience has shown that this system alternates with the attachment system during separation alarms, and the movement in the direction of either system depends upon the intensity of the alarm.

Disorders of this system are generally accompanied by disorders in other psychological systems. This interaction is discussed in greater detail in Chapter III dealing with patternings on the Separation Anxiety Test. At this point it suffices to state that the personality constructs and diagnostic categories adopted by the mental health professions, and generally listed in diagnostic manuals, occasionally recognize disorders in this area. It is likely that diagnosis could be improved if systems such as attachment and self-reliance (individuation) are given adequate consideration.

The Fear-Anxiety-Pain System

During the first year of life the development of the system of reaction to threat of, or actual internal or external, stress increases with the increase in attachment. With increasing attachment the threat of loss produces heightened fear, anxiety, and pain. This observation has been made so consistently by so many observers and is so well-documented that it hardly needs repetition (in primates, Harlow, 1970; Suomi, 1972; in humans, Ainsworth, 1979; Konner, 1977; Mahler, 1968; and others.) As both fear and anxiety become more available as affective reactions, they are soon accompanied by visceral distress. Thus fear, anxiety, and bodily pain (Cannon, 1929) are so closely allied that one is rarely seen without the other when stress occurs.

The fear-anxiety-pain system is readily activated by threats of the loss of familiar surroundings, including persons, places, or things. Kagen (1978) and Mahler (1968) place the period of the most ready onset of this system in relation to the maternal figure toward the last four months of the first year of life. In reviewing the studies in this area Bowlby (1973) suggests a slightly different formulation in which the onset is not sudden but is rather a gradual movement from the distress of the first three months, to wariness of the next three, and finally to what is more recognizable as fear in the following months. The term separation anxiety was developed to describe this phenomenon. However, fear of strange persons and objects, which does appear definitely in the latter part of the first year, is highly related to separation anxiety and, of course, to the attachment system. This system of reactivity is not only a developmental phenomenon, but continues to play an important role throughout the life cycle. It is survival based and is generally considered to be instinctive.

Although Bowlby has ascribed protection as the main function of the attachment system, it is also true that the separation pain system has a similar function. It is a stress system producing a need to seek relief and usually resulting in an effort toward homeostasis. Fear, anxiety, and pain (visceral distress) require some form of intrapsychic as well as behavioral reactivity to arrive at a balance of safety. Most authors and researchers have been concerned with this phenomenon as a precursor of a search for safety. Threats and actual traumatic events are considered to be the arousers of this system. Although it has not been referred to as a psychological system, yet, considering that these affects are known to be developmental and universal, it seems difficult not to conceive of this complex as a system.

The Hostility System

The hostility system has its onset mainly in the second year of life but under pathological circumstances can develop earlier in the first year. It follows closely on the heels of the fear-anxiety-pain system. Its primary function is to attack a real or an imagined aggressor, depriver, or frustrator for the purpose of retrieving or simply obtaining the object, the experience, the person, or the place that was either lost, threatened, needed, or taken. In the psychoanalytic field it was often held that the system evolves out of the death instinct (Klein, 1948) and that it is the precursor of anxiety. Studies of development have shown that this concept is mistaken and that satisfactory development of the attachment system, which is more primary, acts as a controlling force over this system (Harlow, 1970; Bowlby, 1973). The availability of a significant attachment figure with a strongly benign influence prevents the system of hostility from controlling other major psychological systems.

In separation situations hostility may have a significant role, but under most circumstances it is not dominant. When separation situations become severely threatening or intensely depriving, however, severe rage may be induced for a period of time (Wolfenstein, 1969). Separation experiences generally bring other systems into more dominant positions. The reasons appear to lie largely in the wish to retain the caring by an attachment figure who sets the limits for the use of the hostility system. In later life the model of such a figure becomes a strong element of the personality (in psychoanalysis, cathected). In classical psychoanalytic theory the good attachment figure (usually maternal) is incorporated or internalized. Through the medium of the good attachment figure the limits to the use of the hostility system have been set. If the attachment figure has been unable to set the necessary limits (especially those of the particular culture), the child may proceed to test these limits until they are set by someone else in the family or in the community.

Hostility aroused by separation (Hansburg, 1972) has been referred to as separation hostility precisely because it is referrable to a threat of, or an actual loss of, an attachment figure or a very familiar place or object. Further, separation hostility does reach an autonomous role in many personalities so that it can be aroused immediately without necessarily being accompanied by an awareness of the fear-anxiety-pain system. Although this system of reactivity does have autonomy on a developmental basis, it is integrally related to other psychological systems for the purpose of relieving pressure on any of them. Yet when it is serving various systems, the manner in which it is being used may vary considerably. For example, hostility in the service of the attachment system may be used to injure anyone who attempts to separate an individual from an attachment figure. On the other hand, hostility in the service of individuation (self-reliance) may resist the aid of supportive persons during a separation experience.

The Defensive System

The human organism is equipped with a propensity for developing various patterns of reaction that defend it against the full impact of an unpleasant or a disturbing experience. The capacity for defense is available to the organism very early in development. Bowlby (1962) suggests that defensive patterns may also develop at later stages of life to serve varied purposes. More recently, Bowlby (1980) has developed a theory of defense related to information processing. In his new theoretical framework he utilizes the concept of defensive exclusion of information as a substitute for the concept of repression. Similar to repression he conceives of this process as unconscious, as extremely rapid, and as the basis for pathology. Moreover, he suggests that there is a cognitive aspect to defense, which he refers to as defensive belief, and a behavioral aspect, which he calls defensive behavior.

Further, Bowlby (1980) suggests that defensive exclusion may eventually result in the deactivation of a psychological system, for example, attachment. His theory, supported by the observations of Peterfreund (1971), leads to the conclusion that information which has previously led to considerable unhappiness and suffering is defensively excluded. Thus, in relation to separation experiences, defensive exclusion may lead to the reduction of either fear, hostility, or self-reliance. Not only is this true of childhood, but, as has been demonstrated in victims of concentration camps or in the brain-washing experiments of the various secret service agencies in many countries, deactivation of certain psychological systems can occur in adults of varying ages.

Clinical and research evidence suggests that defensive exclusion is essential to survival. Very few individuals experience life in their culture without occasionally having to face stimuli so overwhelming that they cannot adequately be processed without severe blows to the integration of the psychological systems of the personality. Degrees of defensive exclusion then become necessary. Sometimes these are adaptive and successful and sometimes maladaptive, limiting certain systems in their functioning. This is implied by Bowlby (1980) in his discussion of defensive exclusion; the present discussion is extended to systems other than the attachment system.

Separation experiences during childhood often produce defensive beliefs as well as defensive behavior. The gradual exclusion of separation stimuli that may endanger the safety of the organism may eventually extend to very minor stimuli, such as the movement of the mother from one part of the room to another. The defensive belief may then consist of denial that the mother moved at all, especially if the mother continues to be unaccepting of both the attachment and the pain system of the child. On the other hand, denial may consist of ignoring the mother if she comes to talk to the child, a species of defensive behavior.

It has been pointed out (Hansburg, 1972) that heightened defensive development in relation to separation from attachment figures (previously referred to as reality avoidance and/or separation denial) is more characteristic of pathology, yet to some degree is essential for ego survival. The Separation Anxiety Test is very sensitive to pathology of the defensive system.

The Self-Evaluative System

While the ego (self) requires considerable development before full self-evaluation occurs, there is much evidence that profound effects on the self-evaluative system occur very early in infancy. The accessibility and regularity of the maternal figure provide the organism with a feeling of well-being and a good homeostasis. This organismic feeling permeates the psychological systems as they develop, and balances their functioning. In a sense the child's self-evaluation becomes the degree to which he has experienced a meaningful evaluation by significant attachment figures. These experiences form the unconscious substratum of his future self-evaluation.

The self-evaluation system may be conceived as consisting of three sub-systems.

1. The self-love system, a primary experiential phenomenon related to being loved and therefore feeling lovable and capable of being loved.

2. The self-esteem system, a secondary state related to success in exploratory behavior.

3. The sense of identity, the feeling of who or what one is and related to one's place in the community or tribe.

These subsystems form a complex of self-awareness, which is then related to self-care. In psychoanalytic theory, the term narcissism has been used to encompass these systems and is one of the most widely used concepts developed by Freud and his followers. Since the term was originally intended to refer to the physical image of the self and was later extended to the mental and emotional image of the self, it has been standard in most psychological theory and practice.

Because the term self-love may have many connotations, it may be easily misunderstood and misinterpreted. To love the self may imply values that are self-oriented rather than morally or socially oriented. Yet the evidence from clinical and personal historical data has strongly suggested that self-love is definitely and positively related to experiences of being wanted, loved, and cared for by an attachment figure, usually the mother. Such experiences build self-acceptance or self-love within the limits of the moral and social milieu. Self-love is used here to connote the experience of being loved and therefore feeling loved. Perhaps it can be rephrased in personal terms as follows: "I love myself because I am and have been loved and cared for and therefore I am lovable and capable of being loved by others." With such an unconscious frame of reference, love may then more easily be manifested toward others. Blanton (1956) expressed this point as follows: " Love also means love of self. This is an aspect often ignored, yet it is of basic importance—for without healthy self-love, one cannot love anyone else." White (1963) has a very penetrating discussion of self-love as it contrasts with self-esteem.

The self-esteem system is much more conscious and derives largely from experiences in the effectiveness of exploratory behavior and in the manipulation of the environment. It is this feeling of being effective or competent which is fundamental to the concept of self-esteem and is referred to by White (1963) as the feeling of effectance. References to this concept may be found in Hansburg (1972).

The self-love and self-esteem systems finally merge with a social role and a third system, which we can refer to as "identity." Who or what the individual feels he is in relation to others represents this third subsystem of self-evaluation.

Separation experiences often affect the systems of self-evaluation. Unfavorable effects on these systems, especially the system of self-love, is found in depression, self-deprecating behavior, masochism, self-destructiveness, and suicide. Although infancy is the period in which traumatic separations or arbitrary accessibility of the maternal figure is most likely to result eventually in weaknesses in all three systems, later separations or traumatic deprivations of attachment figures may seriously weaken the processes of these systems. It has been demonstrated that experiences in concentration camps have seriously undermined all or anyone of these systems (Niederland, 1968).

Summary of Psychological Systems and Separation

The six psychological systems (one of which includes three subsystems) referred to cursorily are believed to be of greatest significance in relation to separation experiences. Not mentioned are other psychological systems of importance to human personality and behavior—for example, the sexual system. The basic reason for this omission lies in the fact that because the Separation Anxiety Test was developed for children, complicated problems would arise in trying to elicit responses in this area. The systems described have been found to be intimately associated with separation problems and therefore of most value in a study of separation disorders.

The psychological systems or processes mentioned are each represented by unconscious movements of sensory and perceptive experiences, each consisting of memory stores of episodic and semantic nature, each manifesting itself unconsciously to the hierarchial self, and each manifesting itself in behavioral forms. The total organism that provides the equipment for these processes to operate may, depending upon the nature and extent of experience, undergo cycles of chemical and structural change as a result of malfunction or deactivation of a psychological system (Bowlby, 1980; see also, McKinney, 1971, 1973).* In separation disorders we are dealing with dysfunctional patterns that may not only penetrate all psychological systems but may also involve chemical changes in internal somatic or physiological processes.

Once we conceive of a separation disorder as a dysfunctional, pathological patterning of interacting psychological systems, we can arrive at a picture of maladaptive personality functioning by a study of the combinations of patterns obtained from the Separation Anxiety Test. The degree and nature of the disorder may be determined by the extent of the disturbance within each system as well as by the dysfunctional relationship between them. For example, if the attachment system is too readily awakened by minor separation stimuli and is more readily awakened by such stimuli than the individuation (self-reliance) system, the separation disorder is more severe than if the total attachment reactions are especially strong. Further, the more localized the system disturbance and the less disturbances in the other systems, the more likelihood that the separation disorder is minor.

In the following section an attempt is made to classify and to describe various patterned separation disorders derived from the Separation Anxiety Test, utilizing the psychological systems discussed. The difficulty of this task can be appreciated when it is recognized that conventional nosology includes a long-standing vocabulary of pathology. This vocabulary has been so thoroughly engendered in the day-to-day clinical operations of mental health professionals that it is impossible to read any diagnostic study of a child, adolescent, or adult without encountering such diagnostic categories as obsessive-compulsive, hysterical, anxiety neurosis, and the like. For this reason it seems preferable to consider the following disorders as addenda to any other dynamic statements made to characterize an individual's personality, emotional, or behavioral problems.

See bibliography on DeFeudis work on mice.

Anxious Attachment

This term has been borrowed from Bowlby (1973), who has found it highly useful in referring to behavior that manifests the characteristics of anxiety and attachment to a great degree in a separation situation. It is described by him (p. 213) as follows: "Apprehension lest attachment figures be inaccessible and/or unresponsive. For these reasons, therefore, and especially because it can be expected to enlist our sympathy, anxious attachment is the term to be used." Bowlby includes in this category only apprehension that the attachment figure may abandon, may be lost, or in some way be unavailable when needed. In this discussion anxious attachment includes fear of places or objects associated with this inaccessibility and the visceral or other physical distress that may accompany it. All these feelings are so intimately bound with each other that together they form a distressing and disturbing pattern strongly related to attachment need.

On the basis of both research with typical populations of adolescents and adults as well as clinical study with the Separation Anxiety Test, it is postulated here that a pattern of anxious attachment occurs contiguously with threatened separations or serious losses. In individuals relatively free of pathology, many conditions may arise that provide good and sufficient reason for anxious attachment. Serious illness of a loved person, the real danger of accidental loss of an attachment figure, economic or social upheaval endangering the safety of the family, or reports of approaching cataclysms threatening to engulf loved ones—all these are sufficient cause for anxious attachment patterns. The author has found such patterns in individuals of all ages who show no forms of emotional pathology. Mothers of young children will normally show a pattern of anxious attachment on the pictures of the Separation Anxiety Test simply because they are demonstrating their own caretaking behavioral needs. Similarly, such patterns have been found in typical adolescents, older adults, and the elderly.

On the other hand mental health professions are quite familiar with the pathological forms of anxious attachment seen in early childhood, in school children, in adolescents, and in adults. Pathological reactions are postulated whenever anxious attachment appears to be quite inappropriate to the nature of the separation stimulus, whether reality based or spontaneously stimulated by thought referrable to the memory store. Thus, if a mother leaves a room after putting her ten-year-old to bed, it is considered pathological for the child to demonstrate anxious attachment unless some serious threat of danger exists which is not implicit in the mother's departure from the room. The same is true if, because of some frustration during the day, the youngster suddenly feels threatened by abandonment. It is therefore assumed that the threat does not exist at this time in the situation but is a longstanding patterned insecurity within the youngster based upon other experiences and threats of loss only faintly related to the present one. Pathological reactions when elicited by a mild stimulus must necessarily be related to earlier insecurities which are now easily triggered by minor events.

Thus, the discussion distinguishes between varying degrees of anxious attachment, ranging from mild to severe. The Separation Anxiety Test patterns associated with mild anxious attachment consist of high percentages of both attachment and separation pain. This combination of patterns is one of the most typical and readily discernible combinations. Generally, the balance of attachment and individuation (self-reliance) responses are within the normal range, that is, few attachment responses and many individuation (self-reliance) responses on mild pictures and the reverse on strong pictures, with a total attachment percentage higher than the total individuation (self-reliance) percentage. Further, the separation pain percentage is higher than the norms and higher than the percentage of hostility responses. For mild anxious attachment to be present all the other factors in the test must be relatively intact, except possibly for a somewhat lower individuation (self-reliance) percentage.

The presence of this combination should be considered a fairly typical phenomenon and, in fact, has both theoretical and clinical implications. The author has concluded that in order to maintain the mutuality of feeling and the normal proximity between the child and the mother (or other attachment figure) both must be capable of a mild degree of anxious attachment when there are real separation threats. This must be so in order that the instinct of self-preservation in the child and the reciprocal care-taking behavior of the maternal figure remain in mutual operation. Clinically, mild anxious attachment is a healthy sign and should be treated as such.

A somewhat stronger anxious attachment is manifested on the Separation Anxiety Test when, in addition to the pattern of mild anxious attachment, the balance between the attachment system and the individuation (self-reliance) system *on the mild pictures* is reversed, that is, with attachment responses being stronger than the individuation (self-reliance) responses. Further, the total individuation (self-reliance) percentage is below the norms. Another significant addition is a strong rise in the percentage of responses in the defensive system (which include withdrawal evasion and fantasy). The addition of this factor indicates an increasing intensity of efforts to avoid the impact of the separation by any of the techniques of intrapsychic or behavioral defensive maneuvers. Bowlby (1980) refers to this process as exclusion of unpleasant episodic or semantic memories no doubt associated with the depicted separation. In this test it has been characterized as a disorder of the defensive system. A further characteristic of strong anxious attachment is the high level of both the pain and hostility sytems, that is, more than 30 percent of the responses in this area.

Severe anxious attachment may be posited if, in addition to the above, the self-evaluative systems are disturbed. This may be shown by two significant factors: (1) the self-love loss is considerable and is higher in percentage of responses than preoccupation with self-esteem; (2) there is either a paucity of responses to identity stress or an exaggerated number of them. Our experience has shown that when there is greater concern with being loved and wanted than with intellectual or environmental operations on the test, a definite depressive factor is added to anxious attachment. As previously noted, feeling loved and wanted by others and by the self represents a more profound and more primary need, and its failure of gratification indicates a serious dysfunction of the self-evaluative system.

When severe anxious attachment is present, it has been suggested that an *unconscious symbiotic need* exists (Hansburg, 1972, 1976). This need may be defined as an intense unconscious wish for the kind of relationship in which the individual feels fully and completely attached to an attachment figure. It resembles *symbiosis* as defined in biology but only symbolically and is not necessarily shared by an attachment figure. Bowlby (1974) believes that the term is not happily chosen, because it refers to the adaptive partnership in which both parties need each other for survival. Nevertheless, it is possible for an individual to be unconsciously seeking to establish this kind of relationship, which, of course, is unrealistic, and for this reason the individual is bound to be constantly frustrated. The term has been utilized quite valuably by Benedek (1949) and Mahler (1968), especially in connection with infantile psychosis. The present use of this term refers mainly to an unconscious feeling related to unassuaged experiences during the period of early childhood when the mother's need to separate from the infant for some periods was never adequately accepted by the child. This need becomes incorporated into the attachment pattern, acted out symbolically and later intensified as a severe anxious attachment pattern.

The significance of severe anxious attachment should never be underestimated. It is a serious pathological sign of severe uncertainty in the capacity to achieve loving from an attachment figure. It may well be accompanied by severe feelings of stress and volatile emotional ambivalence. Further, in cases of this kind, self-destructive, masochistic, or suicidal behavior may result if a serious crisis involving attachment figures occurs. These forms of behavior may sometimes result under milder forms of attachment disappointments or separations. The kind of reactions in cases of severe anxious attachment may be more readily discerned from an examination of the dominant response in a given pattern. For example, if in the defensive process system, evasion is a frequent response, we may suspect that the individual will attempt to suppress his agitation and behave as though he were indifferent to his own agitation. Another example is the strength of the intrapunitive response. Our experience indicates that such response will result in guilty and masochistic behavior. Nevertheless, neither of these various behavioral patterns need obfuscate the primary condition of severe anxious attachment.

In other cases abusive or even homicidal behavior may alternate with intense feelings of attachment needfulness. Such behavior may occur in those severe anxious attachment patterns in which hostility is above the norms, even if it does not dominate either the affect picture or the attachment level. The hostility indicates that at the moment the person cannot withstand the inaccessibility or the arbitrariness of the attachment figure. It does not represent the same personality traits as those obtained in severe hostile anxious attachment or in hostile detachment, which are discussed shortly. It merely demonstrates that under separation stress severe attachment needfulness may result in such agitation as to precipitate strong painful and hostile reactions.

As noted above, severe anxious attachment is often accompanied by a weakness of the identity stress response, especially in adolescence. Initially, the identity stress response was thought to be associated with either depersonalization or, at best, a lack of identification with a significant attachment figure. As results of studies with the Separation Anxiety Test have accumulated, it seems likely that in adolescence a low level of responsiveness to this category is associated with difficulty in giving free reign to one's feelings for fear that there will be no return to a more homeostatic condition. In Freudian terminology this refers to a failure of the ability to regress in the service of the ego. In considering this matter from the point of view of attachment theory, it seems more likely that a low level of response represents a fear of change in the self, that is, a fear of the pain of change or growth. That such a fear of change in personality due to separation is associated with strong or severe anxious attachment is understandable.

Hostile Anxious Attachment   50% of our sample have this

Some attachments are fraught with much hostility. This is most notable when the responses to the hostility pattern exceed the norms and especially when they exceed the percentage of separation pain reactions. As Bowlby (1973, p. 247) has stated, anger in separation situations may have two functions: (1) "a forceful reminder that would ensure that the parent would no longer leave him," and (2) "the anger of despair." In bereavement, anger and aggressive behavior are necessarily without function. However, soon the anger is directed at the lost person or against any others who may have been responsible for the loss. Bowlby further states: "Instead of a strongly rooted affection laced occasionally with 'hot displeasure' such as develops in a child brought up by affectionate parents, there grows a deep running resentment held in check only partially by an anxious, uncertain affection." This describes cases of *hostile anxious attachment* in which strong hostility is present and in which it is the dominant affect.

Although Ainsworth (1972, p. 119) has referred to this pattern in very young children as a behavioral system of aggressive angry behavior, she adds that it appears in some infants as "contact resisting behavior." She describes this behavior as follows: "They seek to gain and maintain contact, and they also resist it. They seek to be picked up by the mother, but then hit, kick or push away from her; if put down, they tend to resist release and struggle to gain contact again. Ambivalent responses of this sort are common in young children returning home after separations."

This pattern combination seen in some protocols on the Separation Anxiety Test refers mostly to youngsters whose attachment to their parents is not only filled with uncertainty but is also permeated by intense mutually provoking interactions. The attachment appears to be maintained either by open aggression, provoking comments, seeking each other out for the purpose of argument and dissension, or covert hostility, even in some close families. Yet the attachment is so intense that the family members do not wish to separate from one another even while making efforts to do so. In these cases we see high attachment percentages as well as hostility, in addition to the previously mentioned characteristics of anxious attachment. In classical psychoanalytic literature this pattern is often referred to as sadomasochistic interaction.

In some cases there is evidence of severe anxious attachment, but hostility is still high. The evidence, as stated in Hansburg (1972) indicates that a larger percentage of pain responses has been converted to hostility than is found in typical records (see Chapter IV, case 3). This does not mean that such individuals are incapable of agitation or depression during significant separations, threats of loss, or actual loss. It does indicate that the most immediate response is hostility, aggression, or acting out. The major difference is that hostile, aggressive acting out is, for these individuals, the dominant mode of reaction, whereas the counterpart with dominant pain is more likely to react with self-immolation, panic, or depression. In the latter, the effort to retrieve or avenge is more likely to be felt as hopeless or useless; in the former there is greater confidence in the success of aggression. The effort to obtain or maintain closeness is constantly being secured with hostile, provoking reactions.

If the hostility levels dominate all patterns, more serious impulsive aggression is present. In anxious attachment cases where this is true, the attachment figure would easily become the victim of this behavior. If the attachment level is still typical or strong, severe impulsive aggression will be followed by severe guilt. The reasons for this are combinations of disorders of the attachment system, developmental failures in the control of impulse by the attachment system, and efforts at defensive exlusion of the pain system. The mother's (or surrogate caretaker's) separation disorder prevents more typical cultural limit setting, and the usual developmental sequence of the hostility system attains ascendant (DeLozier, 1979). The evidence in both human and nonhuman primates demonstrates that healthy attachment and positive feelings with regard to the accessibility of an attachment figure act as significant mediators, modifiers, and controllers of the later development of aggression. Although S. Freud (1915, 1926) associated aggression with the conflict between profound instinctual necessity and cultural training—largely anal discipline (Klein, 1949, picked up Freud's preoccupation with the death instinct), the evidence indicates that aggression definitely appears developmentally in the second year of life. It is the failure of the security of the attachment figure that permits the uncontrollable unleashing of the hostility system. The latter concept is consistent with clinical observations, suggesting that adequate security with an attachment figure promotes greater impulse control. In psychotherapy we are constantly aware that the resolution of hostility is far more attainable in individuals who are, by early experience, able to transfer to the therapist sufficient positive attachment.

Hostile Detachment

It appears to be theoretically sound that a dominant hostility pattern over a lower attachment pattern represents a serious absence of control of aggression during separation experience. This is true not only when severe anxious attachment is present, but also when increasing detachment appears. Recent experience with adult patterns on the Separation Anxiety Test (DeLozier, 1979) indicates that hostile detachment patterns are characterized by attachment percentages below the norms, individuation (self-reliance) above attachment percentages, high separation hostility, and strong defensive processes. This pattern has been shown to be present more often in abusive mothers than in typical mothers. Thus hostile detachment differs from hostile anxious attachment because of the drop below the norms of the attachment pattern.

The phenomenon of detachment has been studied in early childhood, adolescence, and adulthood. Commenting on detachment problems in early childhood, Heinicke and Westheimer (1966) noted the occurrence in some children after brief separations and subsequent reunion with the mother. This detachment at that age was generally found to be temporary and was then followed by behavior designed to increase attachment and to induce the maternal figure not to leave. Thus, after a period this temporary detachment yielded to a return to more typical forms of relationship. In very severe separations of either traumatic or prolonged nature or of an unpredictable character, detachment may set in on a very prolonged or permanent basis. Bowlby (1973) comments that sometimes severe ambivalence sets in, but that detachment may well become a more permanent and relatively fixed pattern of human relationships.

Severe traumatic deprivations such as isolation (McKinney, Harlow and Suomi, 1971) at later stages of development, including adult life, have been known to create a state of detachment. Concentration camp experiences have produced similar forms of detachment. Other forms of artificial tactics have been known to produce forms of detachment. One may infer that severe traumatic events may deactivate the attachment system in the same manner that physical disease may deactivate a physiological system, such as cardiovascular, intestinal, glandular, and the like. Experience has shown that such deactivation of a system may or may not be permanent, depending upon the developmental stage at which the problems occurred and the severity and length of time of deactivation (Bowlby, 1980).

One of the characteristics of detachment is an excessive self-sufficiency. This can be seen on the Separation Anxiety Test when a significant drop in the attachment percentage is accompanied by a high or very high percentage of individuation (self-reliance) responses. The picture suggests the "false self" discussed by Winnicott (1958), described by Schaffer (1968), and further elaborated on the Separation Anxiety Test by Hansburg (1972). When accompanied by high percentages of hostility, this type of detachment is a definite indication of an acting-out personality.

When detachment of the latter type is also accompanied by disturbance of the self-evaluative system, especially in the area of self-love loss, then separation experiences may well produce an alternation between self-sufficiency and depression.

Most detachment problems may be classified as psychopathic or character disordered as long as the number of inappropriate or absurd responses are within normal limits. If a detachment pattern is accompanied by many inappropriate reactions, a probable psychotic acting-out disturbance is present. Generally, most such individuals tend to act out their conflicts, and they show an exaggerated defensive system. They are not good candidates for insight therapy.

The author's own data suggest that hostile, detached persons are often defended by evasion and withdrawal on the Separation Anxiety Test, and for this reason would rarely subject themselves to forms of insight therapy. The attachment level is often quite weak and unstable and is easily overwhelmed by hostility. This is far less true of those who show a pattern of hostile anxious attachment in which the need for attachment is typical or high and separation pain is strong.

Dependent Detachment

In a small percentage of adolescents and adults, responses to the attachment and individuation (self-reliance) patterns fall below the norms. Our clinical experience suggests that when this occurs, it represents a very poor resource level. The author has also referred to this phenomenon as very poor personality core strength. Both significant systems have been deactivated and indicate a general impoverishment of the personality. The person possesses limited capacity to form a reciprocal attachment relationship and also shows a poor exploratory behavioral system. Such persons are likely incapable of managing their affairs or daily life tasks with any consistency or reliability. They remain highly dependent upon others but resist closeness when it requires giving of themselves. Their commitments are generally dubious and unreliable, and they are not likely to remain for any length of time at any kind of work or service. Even if they remain committed, they will tend to be late or absent and to pay minimal attention to their tasks.

Along with this low resource level we often see high levels of impulsive and poorly controlled affect, generally dominated by fear and anxiety but at times also by strong hostility. The activation of these systems is obviously a sign of helplessness since they are easily aroused when the sources of dependency gratification are threatened while coping resources are poor. In such a case patterns of defensive processes are generally dominated by evasion. When this characteristic is combined with a low resource level and high affect, we can expect that persons with such patterns will be difficult to handle. Chronic devious behavior can be expected.

Because true attachments are so tenuous for such persons, they most readily accept relationships that are of the caretaking variety and for as long as the caretaker provides security. If another caretaker appears who will provide equivalent or better care, their allegiance will readily shift to that figure. Thus, their relationships are unreliable and unstable, affect-ridden, and highly dependent upon narcissistic gratifications.

In psychoanalytic work these individuals have been variously referred to as immature personalities, infantile, dependent characters, narcissistically dependent persons, or even borderline characters. If we utilize Bowlby's attachment theory in understanding these people, we might well study the nature of their early experiences with caretaking figures. Examinations of histories of such persons indicate that parental behavior had generally been neglectful and arbitrarily superficial. Devious behavior in the parents was found to be quite common and was accordingly encouraged in the children. Generally the children went their own way, because the parents were largely concerned with their own narcissistic gratifications. In some cases the fathers were inadequate persons, given to gambling or other forms of sociopathic behavior, and the mothers were either emotionally inaccessible or arbitrary. This form of pathological attachment experience seems to carry with it poor development of personal adaptive resources.

The pattern just described is not solely or exclusively the type of pattern resulting from the above experiences but it is a significant one. In some cases the pattern of anxiety, fear, and pain is exceedingly strong, and the detachment is characterized by severe panic if a caretaking figure is lost. Despite this panic, the basis for the attachment still remains highly dependent and narcissistic, with little or no concern for the real welfare of the caretaker.

Excessive Self-Sufficiency

This characteristic has been previously referred to as common in individuals with inadequate attachment patterns, such as in hostile detachment. It can be a pattern of its own in cases in which the attachment level is within normal limits. The pattern is much more common than dependent detachment and is characterized by high or very high levels of individuation (self-reliance) responses and definitely far higher than the attachment level. The individuation (self-reliance) responses are often especially frequent on the strong separation pictures, and the balance with attachment on both mild and strong pictures is the reverse of that seen in severe anxious attachment. The reason appears to lie in the strong confidence such people have in their ability to seem at ease with strong separations. However, when such confidence is stronger than the need for the attachment figure under circumstances in which the emotionally healthy tendency is a need for closeness, excessive self-sufficiency must be posited.

In many cases of this kind there is often a hostility level higher than typical and stronger than pain. When both of these appear, we are confronted with an acting-out person with excessive self-sufficiency. In order to diagnose such a person as an aggressively acting-out, excessively self-sufficient person, it is essential that both individuation (self-reliance) responses and hostility be the strongest percentages in the total protocol.

Theoretically and clinically a combination of hostility and self-sufficiency is a sine qua non of the aggressive acting-out person. Such individuals tend to pursue life styles that dominate others and control through manipulation and/or aggression rather than through positive feeling and understanding of others. They are often quick to assert themselves in situations that do not require assertion and which are often dysfunctional in relation to any constructive purpose. The acquisition of such personality traits is not within the purview of this book. It has been well covered by others.

When the pattern of self-love loss is stronger and higher than the self-esteem preoccupation level and is combined with the above pattern, a definitely masochistic element is added. Usually, however, this aspect of the protocol is not present and the general picture is that of aggressive dominance. Guilt is not a common characteristic of individuals in this category.

Further, our data from the Separation Anxiety Test indicate that defensive processes stay in the background in these cases. This suggests that both typical and intense separation experiences do not awaken enough attachment feeling in these persons to require significant defensiveness. They too readily express resentments and assertiveness and therefore have less need for withdrawal, evasion, or fantasy. They are generally very realistic and show few absurd responses.

The Depressive Syndrome   100 %

This syndrome has been mentioned in relation to the psychological system of self-evaluation. Further, it has been suggested that the syndrome is most common in cases of severe anxious attachment, although it may occur in other categories. The response area that tends to be most involved in this syndrome is self-love loss (feelings of rejection and intrapunitiveness). Strong responsiveness to this area, especially when it exceeds the self-esteem preoccupation area, is pathognomic of a depressive trend in the personality. When it is integrally involved with severe anxious attachment, there is likely to be strong self-destructive fantasies or behavior. Attempted suicide is often seen in persons who show this pattern (Hansburg, 1976). The author has recently been able to substantiate this factor in the elderly (Hansburg, 1980), and DeLozier (1979) has done so in abusive mothers.

Studies based on different points of view have indicated variously the sources and nature of depression: feelings of helplessness, low levels of self-evaluation, disparity between the actual self and the idealized self, severe guilt feelings in relation to parental figures, profound feelings of loneliness, hostile feelings toward an introjected parental figure that is felt to be alien to the self (Brown, 1974, Brown, Tirril, and Copeland, 1977; Scott and Senary, 1973; and Seligman, 1975). Family histories show the likelihood of loss of a parental figure early in life as well as other sorts of inaccessibility of attachment figures. These factors have been so incorporated in the Separation Anxiety Test as to be readily obtained from certain comparative scores.

For the purposes of this section, listed below is each factor on the Separation Anxiety Test that is diagnostic both of severe anxious attachment and of depression.

1. A stronger attachment than individuation (self-reliance) response percentage *on mild pictures.*

2. A below-average percentage of individuation (self-reliance) responses on all pictures.

3. More than 30 percent responses to the total of pain and hostility reactions.

4. A high level of defensive processes (referred to as reality avoidance or separation denial).

5. A strong level of self-love loss—more than 8 percent and higher than self-esteem preoccupation.

6. A weak level of identity stress. (This has been found less useful with adults.)

A combination of these six factors with poor reality testing—more than the usual number of inappropriate or absurd responses —probably indicates a propensity to psychotic and delusional forms of depressiveness and self-destructiveness.

Because the preceding pattern may be interpreted as longstanding depression rather than an adjustment reaction, we may infer that all of the major psychological systems previously discussed are in a state of considerable turmoil. Minor separation threats may precipitate depression.

The Separation Anxiety Test does readily distinguish between long-standing, chronic depressive trends and depressions that may normally occur as a result of common life frustrations and disappointments. The distinction may be seen when we compare minor variations in the self-evaluative systems with the degree of intensity of disturbance in the other psychological systems interpreted from the test. Thus, if the attachment, individuation (self-reliance), pain, and hostility systems are within normal limits, it is obvious that any depressive trend is mild and occasional rather than strong and frequent. Further, the nature of the depressive trend may be ascertained from a study of the patterning of the affected psychological systems.

Depression, like other pathologically psychological systems, is a symptom of some disturbance in the unconscious processes and in the unconscious self. In most individuals it should not be considered a disease. As noted previously, a variety of intrapsychic or situational antecedents operate together with deficiencies in the various psychological systems. These antecedents must be considered as precipitants of depression, varying with each individual and at different times in the same individual. In the Separation Anxiety Test it has been both hypothecated and authenticated that separations often produce depressive reactions that are manifested in the self-evaluative system. Nevertheless, separations are only one of the causes of depressive reactions, although a significant cause.

Summary

This discussion has presented certain significant patterned separation disorders that frequently appear on the Separation Anxiety Test. Included are anxious attachment, mild, strong, and severe, hostile anxious attachment, hostile detachment, dependent detachment, excessive self-sufficiency, and depressive syndrome. These patterns have been interpreted in terms of intactness or disturbance of the psychological systems previously discussed. Although the general and detailed material of this method can be subsumed under Bowlby's (1969) attachment theory, much material is derived from observations made in psychoanalytic formulations, such as those inferred from Mahler (1968).

Further, *Separation Disorders* have been defined as patterns of dysfunctioning or pathological psychological systems. Recognition of these disorders can be of considerable value to any mental health professional who needs to diagnose, to make recommendations for, or to treat human emotional disturbances.

The succeeding chapters contain the detailed analyses of scores on various items and patterns of the Separation Anxiety Test, with case presentations. Those psychologists who wish to use the test should study the material carefully as a guide to the analysis of a test protocol.

CHAPTER

II

INTERPRETATION OF RESPONSE FREQUENCY
ON THE SEPARATION ANXIETY TEST METHOD

Introduction

Interpretation is a complex process demanding not only clinical experience and skill, and knowledge of a person's background, but also a thorough understanding of the psychological instrument. Levy (1963, p. 157) describes this process as follows:

> Psychodiagnosis is a descriptive venture having as its ultimate goal the provision of a basis for the anticipation of the behavior of the patient under various contingencies. Unless it can be shown that this goal is accomplished by the use of a particular psychodiagnostic approach, continued use of that approach represents sheer ritual. Therefore, if the technician is not to be found guilty of engaging in ritualistic behavior in the pursuit of his academic goals, he must be able to demonstrate that the product of this psychodiagnostic procedure permits predictions to be made about a patient's behavior at a higher level of accuracy than could otherwise be obtained.

With additional acumen Rosenzweig (1949, pp. 2-3) notes:

> It is recognized that empirical signs alone can provide a basis for scientifically investigating and predicting behavior. It thus becomes the task of psychodiagnosis to bridge the gap between diagnostic indications and implicit psychodynamic forces—an objective that must depend largely on new knowledge of the systematic relationship between the various levels of the personality.

The weaving of the various facets of the Separation Anxiety Test Method into a total personality reaction pattern of separation experiences can best be accomplished if the psychologist sharpens his observation of the various factors in the test as well as of the meaning of the obtained patterns. To arrive at such an insight leading to justifiable conclusions about any given individual, the psychologist must utilize both the theorietical framework presented in Chapter I, the many different characteristics of the Separation Anxiety Test Method, his own clinical experience and training, and the case material presented in this work.

As pointed out in Volume I the interpretation of this test method depends on studying the frequency of responses to the total protocol, to individual responses, to response patterns, and to the relationship between all these. This chapter deals with the interpretation of the frequency responses to the total examination, to the mild and strong pictures, to the individual pictures, and to items selected by various youngsters during the course of examination. Although some material may be repeated from Volume I, much of it will elaborate on the material of that volume.

Interpretation of the Total Responses

Generally speaking, the total number of responses to many projective tests has some significant diagnostic value but there are serious limits to such significance. The Separation Anxiety Test Method is not any different in this respect. The number of responses may be so limited that the only interpretation is an inner resistance or fear of cooperation lest the individual reveal something that is too threatening. There are 204 possible responses, and in the author's experience with the instrument any protocol containing less than 20 responses is almost useless for meaningful interpretation. Since the median hovers around 57, responses between 20 and 40 have to be considered as a constricted record.

Constricted responsiveness is a familiar concept to psychologists working with projective tests so it needs very little elaboration here. Youngsters with acting-out characterological disorders tend to respond in this manner, although it is also true that emotionally impoverished individuals or those who have been severely traumatized will also give few responses. On the other hand a very large number of responses, 100 or more, are given by obsessional individuals who, because of ambivalence, want to include as much as they can in order to feel a sense of achievement. For them the test method becomes an immediate challenge to their self-esteem. In many cases the Separation Anxiety Test Method is highly stimulating and results in a greater degree of responsiveness than other types of projective tests. It is obvious that no experienced psychologist would make definitive diagnostic judgments on the basis of the total number of responses, but the latter does have some meaning once the entire protocol has been studied.

As indicated in Volume I, the total number of responses may readily be influenced by the method of examination. An experiment dealing with the method of answering "yes" or "no" to each statement was discussed on page 48 of Volume I. Other statements altering the directions are likely to influence the total number of responses as well. Such directional alterations often result in increasing responses on most projective tests. For example, if the examiner suggests to the youngster that most other people give many more responses, a definite spurt will occur. It has been the author's experience with this instrument that efforts to increase the number of responses by forms of stimulation not intended in the development of the method may nullify its usefulness.

Responses on Mild and Strong Pictures

For interpretive purposes the Separation Anxiety Test is divided into two equal parts, mild pictures (2, 3, 4, 5, 7, 9) and strong pictures (1, 6, 8, 10, 11, 12). (See Volume I) The number of responses to each group in relation to each other has much more significance than the total number of responses. Since one of the basic premises of this test method is the relatonship between the strength of the separation stimulus and the type and frequency of the responses, we would expect that the strong pictures would produce greater response frequency and more intense responses. It is very rare indeed to find a record in which the number of responses on the strong pictures is less than that on the mild pictures. Generally the percentage of responses to the strong pictures is 60 percent and to the mild pictures, 40 percent, a difference of 20 percent. Any noticeable lessening of this difference should be subject to careful scrutiny, to determine where in the protocol there has been an increase in the responses to the mild pictures or where there has been a decrease in responses to the strong pictures.

Where the total number of responses to the mild pictures is very close to that of the strong pictures or approximately equal, an obvious degree of pathology is present. The pathological significance of this reaction lies in the increasing degree of insensitivity and poor judgment with regard to the strength of the stimulus. The condition may be found in some cases of severe anxious attachment, but is more common in hostile detachment as well as in dependent detachment. On the whole this symptom is generally found in a more detachment-oriented individual because of its symptomatic insensitivity.

Differences between 20 and 30 percent between the strong and the mild pictures have a healthier significance and are more common in youngsters with good strong attachments to their families. Nevertheless, when the percentage of difference rises above 30, indicating few responses to the mild pictures and many responses to the strong pictures, we may be tapping a possible symbiotic factor. The individual is very comfortable under the ordinary circumstances of daily separations but is severely thrown by strong separations. This symptom is much more common in persons who are relatively less resourceful and more anxiously attached when separation demands are strong. Whether or not this problem is acted out or is more depressive in nature, or is both at different times, depends upon the more substantive nature of the actual responses and their relationship to one another.

Theoretically, the degree of sensitivity to separation stimuli seems to be related to the extent to which the child successfully or unsuccessfully negotiated the crucial period of awareness of the existence of the maternal figure outside the realm of sensory perception. The variety of patterns that may result from such an experience is implied in the experimental studies of Ainsworth (1979). It seems likely that in many cases the result of an impermanence or inconstancy of the object or model is a lasting insecurity with regard to the accessibility of the attachment figure.

However, in some cases there may result a lasting sense of certainty that no attachment figure is available. Therefore, one would presume that detachment of this kind is accompanied by increasing insensitivity with regard to separations and that the result on the Separation Anxiety Test includes inadequate differentiation between frequencies of response to mild and strong stimuli. Perhaps this conclusion seems to be a far cry from the behavior of a one- to two-year-old child, but much in later human behavior is motivated by such very early experiences.

If the above is true with regard to response frequency to mild and strong stimuli, it must certainly be true when one examines the type of responses differentiating between such stimuli. Mild reactions such as sublimation, feelings of well-being, and adaptation are generally more frequent on the mild pictures; strong attachment reactions such as loneliness, strong tension reactions such as fear or anxiety, or considerable hostility such as projection or anger are more frequent on the strong pictures. Whenever the reverse occurs, pathology of some type is present; the nature of this pathology depends upon other aspects of the protocol.

Normally, then, the lessened frequency of responses to mild pictures and the heightened frequency of responses to strong pictures, in addition to a greater frequency of strong emotional reactions to the strong pictures and a greater frequency of mild emotional reactions to the mild pictures, provide a more normative frequency setting in which to judge the child's reactions to separation. One of the most diagnostic factors in the Separation Anxiety Test Method is the correlation between the intensity of the separation stimulus and the corresponding quality and frequency of the intensity of the reactions.

Frequencies on Individual Pictures

Ordinarily the pictures yielding the greatest response frequency are the "judge" and the "maternal death" pictures. The least frequency is provided by the "sleep" and "sailor" pictures. Obviously, such frequencies are based upon appropriate responses to the intensity of the stimuli. Whenever a specific picture produces a frequency that is not only larger or smaller than expected but is also disproportionate to the remainder of the protocol, we can be certain that this picture is probably significant to the individual. (For a fuller discussion of responses to each picture, see Hansburg, 1972, Chap. 10.)

Frequency on each picture is a function of total responsiveness. Frequency should therefore be considered in terms of the percentage of the total. Further, because each individual picture is significant to children, it is difficult to gauge the degree of conventionality and/or individuality of the percentages for each picture.

Frequency of Responses to Mental Set Questions

It is helpful to note the degree of frequency with which individuals answer "yes" to the mental set question "Did this ever happen to you?" A small number of responses, only three or four, suggest a person who has experienced very few separations from significant figures in the environment. On the other hand, a large number of responses, eight, nine, or more, suggest a person who has had many separation experiences and has therefore most likely been traumatized. It is also significant to note whether the emphasis in the separation experiences is on the strong pictures rather than on the mild. This would aid in understanding the intensity of the separations to which the person has been exposed. The obtained protocol can then be interpreted in terms of the frequency of such separation experiences without necessarily resorting to the child's history. It is significant to know how often the child has felt separated. If this is in contrast to the history, it would form an interesting interpretation of fantasy life.

Interpretation of Item Frequencies

Seventeen responses are provided for each picture, and each represents a specific mode of emotional and/or behavioral reaction to a separation experience. Since each of the 17 responses appears for each picture, the total frequency for each item on all 12 pictures achieves a degree of significance in relation to the other responses. The items with the greatest frequency take on meaning in relation to behavioral manifestations during separation experiences.

How can we study the item frequencies so that we can derive the greatest clinical benefit? According to our studies with this method, the items of loneliness and its balance partner, adaptation to separation, should generally show the largest number of responses. Feelings of loneliness in the protocol generally aternate with the adaptive response, thus indicating that the respondent may make the best of the situation even if lonely. However, loneliness should appear more frequently in the strong pictures and adaptation more frequently on the mild pictures.

Another strong area is that of empathy, which is usually less in frequency than loneliness but bears a close relationship to it. The implication of the empathy response in the situation is more needful on the side of others than the respondent; that is, others need him more than he needs them. The healthier picture requires that loneliness be more frequent. The rationale for this lies in the capacity to admit that a separation situation stimulates the need for others. The fact that others may need one at such moments more than one needs them is, in a sense, begging the question. It is emotionally more realistic to feel lonely when a person experiences separation than to feel sorry for someone else, although the latter does apply in some situations. Nevertheless, empathy is a facet of attachment, and for the purposes of this test method it is closely allied to it. Further, it is obvious that empathy is expected to be present, if at all, on the strong pictures and rarely present on the mild ones.

Anxiety and fear (phobic) responses are expected to be rather well distributed among both the mild and the strong pictures. The fear response is so common on this test that when it does not appear at all or appears infrequently, we should suspect a defensive pattern, that is, a denial of fear. This reaction is often associated with the evasion response. It is more common in excessively self-sufficient and/or acting-out personalities. On the other hand, an excessive percentage of fear responses in the face of low percentages in other areas is seen most strikingly in cases of severe anxious attachment, in persons with symbiotic disorders, and in youngsters who have many specific fears and who compulsively avoid people and places because of these fears. Normally, most children, and indeed older persons tend to associate a place with a severe emotional experience. Traumatic separations may induce such a phobic reaction. A few pictures are likely to produce more phobic reactions than others, for example, the judge and the maternal death pictures. Phobic reactions are rare on the sailor picture.

Generalized anxiety is also a very frequent response in the total protocol, almost as frequent as the fear response. It is generally less frequent than the total loneliness response but correlates highly with it. The mild pictures generate much less anxiety than the strong pictures, but the "grandmother" picture, which is listed among the strong stimuli, does not produce the degree of anxiety usually expected. The explanation for this is discussed in Volume I. At the same time the grandmother picture produces frequent loneliness responses. Some youngsters use the anxiety response as an alternate for the fear response. However, when generalized anxiety becomes stronger than the fear response and is accompanied by high levels of loneliness, anxious attachment may be posited. On the other hand, if high anxiety is accompanied by a low attachment level, it can generally be interpreted as an intensification of the fear of narcissistic destruction rather than the fear of the loss of the love object, or as ego anxiety rather than separation anxiety.

The somatic response is the least frequent of the pain responses and one of the lowest of all reported items on the test. When this response becomes excessive, it is a strong indication that separation stress has been converted into bodily pain. This is generally a strong neurotic indicator but it may also be found in a variety of personality structures. The author has rarely found a case in which somatic responses exceeded phobic or generalized anxiety reactions or the attachment need (see Chapter IV, Case 1).

Withdrawal responses are given with surprising frequency by many youngsters as well as adults. As with most of the available responses, they are more frequent on the strong pictures and should not be too frequent on the mild pictures. Generally, the response is a reasonably healthy one, but when it is excessively frequent, it is symptomatic of the inwardization of separation stress. As with other responses, the reason for inwardization is clarified only by comparison with other responses. Withdrawal is considered to be a defensive maneuver, that is, an effort to avoid or ward off the impact of the separation stress. Withdrawal occurs with greatest frequency in cases of severe anxious attachment, hostile anxious attachment, and hostile detachment, but to be of diagnostic signficance in such cases it must be accompanied by high levels in other areas, as previously noted.

Fantasy responses are quite common in the records of normal individuals. When the frequency of this response is excessive, it signifies a form of denial or avoidance which is defensive in a delusional manner. The latter is most often found in cases of severe anxious attachment. Normally, the response is not common on mild pictures, but in some individuals it can appear frequently on the strong pictures. If the response is found on mild pictures, it may be a symptom of depression, especially if accompanied by many intrapunitive or rejection responses. Low frequencies in this area accompanied by high levels of evasion and low levels of attachment are found in persons with strong self-sufficiency trends.

Evasion responses tend to occur with limited frequency especially in normal records and, in fact, may not appear at all. These responses are most common in persons with increasing detachment or acting out. In such cases evasion is an aggressive rather than a passive response. However, in cases of a symbiotic or strong anxious attachment in which many evasion responses are present, the defensive characterological problems result in a more passive acting out, including self-hurting trends. These problems may consist of avoidance of responsibility, overeating, limited participation in family, neighborhood, or school activities, and other behavior. Thus, the presence of many evasion responses needs to be interpreted in relation to the other items of the test. In general, the more evasion responses the more likelihood of a characterological disorder, but the type of such disorder depends upon the other aspects of the test.

The feeling of rejection response is highly related to the loneliness response as well as to general attachment. High frequencies here are strongly related to depression states as well as to grief. If such responses show increasing frequency on mild pictures, it would indicate a high sensitivity to rejection. This would be related to a symbiotic pull and intense attachment need as well as to potential depressive or paranoid states, depending upon the remainder of the test patterning. Low frequencies of rejection responses are generally more normative. Individuals who tend to feel unloved or not lovable will usually give many rejection responses.

In almost all test protocols, responses of anger are generally present to a degree. An excessive percentage of anger responses, especially on the mild pictures, is very common in persons with hostile-anxious attachment and with hostile detachment. Such excesses are theoretically related to the conflict and ambivalence surrounding the presence or absence of the major attachment figure in the early stages of separation development. When hostility moves largely into projection, however, aggressive feelings and behavior become more pathological. Ordinarily there should be very few or no projection responses. When they show high frequency, especially on the mild pictures, we can be definitely suspicious of a strong paranoid trend in the personality. When anger is used as a technique for blaming others, it is definitely a step beyond the normal angry feelings that an individual feels defensively. In some instances projection definitely approaches a seriously absurd situation. This is specifically applicable to pictures 3, 4, and 7 (see Volume I).

The intrapunitive response represents anger, but the individual feels too guilty to express it and it is turned toward the self. Self-punishment is a familiar phenomenon and is a facet of the loss of the feeling of being loved and therefore of self-love. The number of intrapunitive responses should be small, since they represent guilt and masochism. The number of such responses is commonly larger in individuals who tend to become depressed, especially when the rejection responses are also frequent. When the intrapunitive reactions are frequent on the mild pictures, especially if they are inappropriate to the picture content such as 4 and 7, poor reality testing is a likely interpretation. However, it is important to determine what other frequencies in the test patterning this response is associated with. For anger to be turned inward is highly unrealistic on this test, since the pictures rarely suggest this.

Generally, items of frank emotional stress on the Separation Anxiety Test are expected to be more frequent than more defensive reactions. The healthier person should show frank attachment, adaptive, and emotional stress feelings on the test in addition to other characteristics. Failures in these areas are symptomatic of outright emotional disorder or defensive character and personality traits. On the other hand, excessive reactions in these areas are usually symptomatic of unresolved symbiotic or anxious attachment problems. Our normative data have shown clearly how much greater are the defensive traits in separated children, whereas the more overtly symbiotic reactions are less frequent. Symbiotic disorders in separated children may well lead to delusional and severe self-punishing disorders.

The well-being response occurs most frequently on the mild pictures and, if this is the case, should be considered a healthy reaction. The response is most common on pictures, 2, 3, 4, and 5. When there is a high frequency of this response, especially on the strong pictures, we suspect that there is an increasing insensitivity to separation, an excessive self-sufficiency, a trend toward acting-out. Thus, to report a sense of well-being on the judge and death-of-the-mother pictures would certainly indicate a degree of inappropriateness and of poverty in the attachment area. The relative absence of the well-being response in a protocol is most common in anxious attachment cases as well as in hostile anxious attachment and depression.

Sublimation responses are very common on the mild pictures, although they may occasionally appear on a strong picture. Excesses and absences of such responses have similar implications to the well-being responses. High frequencies are seen in excessive self-sufficiency, and low frequencies occur in depression, anxious attachment, and hostile anxious attachment. Normally, a few sublimation responses on the mild pictures indicate that the individual is quite capable of engaging in activity when the separation is mild and unobtrusive.

The response of impaired concentration is strongly associated with anxiety interferences with school, work, or other areas of intellectual operation. High frequencies in this area are more common in youngsters who are school problems and whose intellectual functioning is highly vulnerable to contact deprivation. Many individuals find a need for contact availability essential for concentration on school work or other forms of study. The threat of deprivation of contact with emotionally supportive figures leaves these youngsters vulnerable to separation pain and immediately disrupts concentration. Some individuals are not aware of this need until separations create the inner distress, which produces the loss of thinking capacity. Impaired concentration responses are rare on the mild pictures, but when they occur on these pictures it is an indication of a severe preoccupation with self-esteem and its loss. A few such responses may generally be found on the strong pictures and as such are within normal expectancy. When excessive, there is an indication of a disorder of the self-evaluative process or system.

The identity stress response represents another aspect of the self-evaluative system. In adolescents a low frequency of this response is associated with difficulties in accepting the need for change or forms of behavior in which the individual yields to what has been termed by the psychoanalytic profession "regression in the service of the ego." It suggests problems in the maturation process in various feelings and behaviors, such as the sexual area. Such weaknesses are commonly seen in cases of severe anxious attachment or hostile anxious attachment as well as in depression. On the other hand, youngsters who show high response frequencies in this area tend to have a far different kind of pathology. Here the significance lies in a current potential fragmentation of the ego structure. Mild pictures do not usually stimulate this response; strong pictures such as the judge or the maternal death pictures often yield identity stress responses.

Although the frequency of absurd (inappropriate) responses has been discussed in Volume I (Hansburg, 1972), it is noted here that the number of these responses tends to increase in those individuals who have an unrealistic attitude toward separation experiences. Such responses are found especially in comfortable reactions to severe separation experiences and some uncomfortable or severely disturbed reactions to very mild pictures. For example, a sublimation response to the maternal death picture is obviously highly inappropriate. Such a mild response or relatively oblivious reaction to a severe separation experience represents poor reality testing, and when it occurs frequently, it must be considered as probably psychotic or, as it is often termed, "ego splitting." Inappropriate affect falls into this category. On the other hand, an identity stress reaction to the sleep picture represents a severe reaction to a very mild stimulus. Thus, inappropriateness can be demonstrated by a mild reaction to a strong stimulus or by a severe reaction to a mild one. It is significant to determine whether the absurd responses are more prevalent on the mild or strong pictures, thus indicating whether we are dealing with oversensitivity or with frequent bland affect.

Although the number of responses to each of the 17 items of the test and their relation to one another has some significance, the human personality is too complicated to rely on single items. For this reason it is necessary to combine the items into patterns and evaluate them in relation to psychological systems. Therefore two charts are provided for the scoring system—one for the individual item responses and the other for the patterns. The two charts are presented for each of the cases in Chapter IV but may also be seen on pages 231 and 232 in the Appendix, Tables A-2 and A-3. The following chapter discusses the interpretation of the pattern frequency percentages, their relationship to one another and to the psychological systems, and the separation disorders discussed in Chapter I.

CHAPTER

III

INTERPRETATION OF
PATTERN FREQUENCIES

It has been demonstrated on the Separation Anxiety Test method that patterned relationships provide an excellent understanding of intrapsychic and behavioral reactions. By placing patterns in juxtaposition we derive meaningful insights into how the youngster handles separation experiences. Some patterns are more diagnostic of basic character structure and others are further indications of emotional and behavioral reactions. By studying the interactions between these, we can obtain meaningful interpretations of the youngster's relatedness, self-reliance, use of resources, dominant emotional feelings, reactive behavior, and developmental levels. (Where percentages are referred to in the following sections, consult Table A-1 in the Appendix.)

Attachment Pattern

The most significant and meaningful pattern consists of attachment reactions. The rationale is derived largely from the individual's normal need for essential human support, especially during crises. This is a primary response related to the basic instinctive need for protection and care and is a measure of the attachment system (see Chapter I, p. 3). No doubt learning experience is highly significant in the normal development of this instinctive need. It is well described by Bowlby (1969) and is further elaborated in his paper on attachment theory (1974). The essential quality is expressed in the ability to maintain close relations and at the same time to permit movement away from closeness in an alternating manner. It involves feelings of loneliness, especially under threat of abandonment or loss of the love object, occasional feelings of rejection, and empathic feelings concerning an attachment figure if the latter appears to be unhappy. The pattern of response just described is a significant indicator of the nature of the attachment relationship.

As described by Hansburg (1972, no. 1) the Separation Anxiety Test Method elicits a general attachment percentage of 20 to 25 percent of the total number of responses. Further, the mild pictures are expected to produce a low number of attachment responses; conversely, the strong pictures are expected to produce a greater number of such responses. Any shift in this pattern should be given careful attention. Thus, a near equalization of the two groups is a likely symbiotic indicator. (See Chapter I, pp. 15-16, for the explanation of the use of this term.) Thus, if there are six attachment reactions to the mild pictures and eight such reactions to the strong pictures, a strong symptomatic symbiotic factor is suggested. Generally, the number of attachment reactions to the strong pictures should be approximately 40 percent greater than the responses to the mild pictures.

When the percentage of attachment responses rises above 25 percent, a strong need for closeness is indicated. The nature of this intensity should be studied by considering excessive responses to mild or strong pictures. If both areas are sizable, we must conclude that the need for closeness is always intense no matter how mild or how strong the separation stimulus. Such a high attachment response is consistent with poor functioning in the absence of a feeling of accessibility of a highly supportive figure (Hansburg, 1972, no. 1). The nature of this poor functioning may be in schoolwork, employment, or avocational pursuits. In other individuals this need is for outlets in reality. That is, the individual is constantly successful in recruiting attachment figures in a pleasant, unobtrusive, and positive manner. The difference between successful and unsuccessful searches for closeness may be seen from other patterns in the test, which are described later.

Any noticeable drop in attachment percentage below 20 percent, for example, 15 percent, should be considered pathognomic of poor relatedness and is quite likely to be observed as a failure in establishing closeness. If on the surface the person appears to be warm and friendly, it must be strongly suspected that this behavior is quite superficial and probably a form of manipulative, psychopathic behavior. Sooner or later, such persons can be expected to alienate others by techniques that may be indicated by other patterns in the test. On the other hand, if the mild pictures show few attachment responses, and the strong pictures show many (for example, one on the mild and ten on the strong), a symptom of excessive self-sufficiency appears. If this occurs within the framework of a total low attachment percentage, a movement away from attachment or closeness may be interpreted and referred to as detachment. The problem may be somewhat different if, despite a severe drop in attachment reactions to mild pictures, the percentage of total attachment responses still remains within the norms. In that case, the remainder of the test patterns should be carefully studied for clues to the self-sufficiency disorder.

The attachment pattern in reaction to separation is most often dominated by the loneliness response; the response empathy is second; rejection, third. On the average, the loneliness response is generally given to approximately one-half of the 12 pictures; empathy, one-third; rejection, one-sixth. The proportions as well as the numbers vary with the total number of responses. If the response loneliness is displaced in dominance by the empathy response even if the total attachment percentage is normal, the indications are that the need for closeness will be dominated by behavior which induces others to seek closeness to one-self without gratification. If rejection dominates the pattern, a strong depressive tone should be posited.

As previously described in relation to strong and severe anxious attachment (Chapter I, pp. 15-16), a very significant pathognomic reaction is demonstrated when the attachment responses to the mild pictures exceed the number of individuation (self-reliance) responses to the mild pictures. This is a very strong symbiotic indicator and may be so interpreted in every case regardless of the remainder of the protocol. The author has not known of a single case in which this phenomenon is present and in which the clinical and historical data did not bear out this interpretation. It is likely that other anxious attachment indicators are also present in the test protocol when the above pattern is manifested.

Attachment responses are very highly correlated with separation pain responses, a phenomenon previously referred to as anxious attachment when both systems are represented by many responses. When both systems are at a low point, we may interpret an increasing insensitivity as well as a probable deep-seated defensiveness. It is also likely that when the above two systems are low, hostility and defensive process systems are represented strongly in the protocol.

Attachment reactions may be interpreted in at least three varied ways: (1) need, (2) capacity, and (3) performance. We may assume that all individuals have a capacity for attachment and that learning experiences decrease or intensify the need for protection by an attachment figure. The need is constantly demonstrated in behavior or performance. Attachment behavior or performance and the manner of this performance may be judged in a variety of ways from the test. Capacity for attachment or for forming closeness with others is certainly related to need, but capacity is not necessarily the same. The capacity may be present but the need may vary considerably according to the situation. Performance would then depend upon both capacity and need. What the test appears to suggest in the attachment area is need and capacity, with the assumption that performance will follow in some manner. Other areas of response to the test will suggest the nature of the attachment performance, whether normal, anxious, hostile, or exaggerated in any significant degree or direction.

Individuation Pattern

Individual resourcefulness in managing oneself in separation situations is a variable of great magnitude. Independence is such a highly valued trait in most cultures that most families, schools, recreation centers, and other areas encourage its growth and development. In fact it is often considered of such paramount importance that attachments may be neglected and/or discouraged in the mistaken conception that they hinder personal development.

Yet such use of individual resources is so dependent upon and closely related to attachment that without the latter, the former often develops pathological forms.

Bowlby has described the relationship between attachment and self-reliance as "an elastic band"; others have used the term "approach-avoidance"; the author has referred to this interaction as the "attachment-individuation balance." The concept has been discussed at great length by both Bowlby (1973) and Ainsworth (1979) and has been documented in research as well as in clinical studies. It has been found extremely useful in the Separation Anxiety Test Method.

How does an individual demonstrate resourcefulness during a separation experience? Obviously, the ability to make adjustments, to accept what has occurred (although perhaps with some reservations and unhappiness) is such a measure. Further, after a period of unhappiness, the ability to assume the tasks of life (sublimation) is of importance, and in the end the reestablishment of an internal feeling of well-being is essential to such resourceful behavior. Much will depend upon the relative intactness of the ego and the capacity for achieving gratification from surrogate relationships as well as from life tasks.

The pattern for this behavior on the test is referred to as "individuation," the term used by Mahler (1968), Masterson (1972), and many others in the psychoanalytic field. In Chapter I this term is used with the parenthetic phrase "self-reliance," a term used by Bowlby (1973) with a similar but slightly different connotation. On the test we obtain a higher score in this area on the mild pictures than on the strong pictures. The most dominant response in the pattern is the adaptive reaction to both mild and strong pictures. The sublimation response as well as the well-being response occurs largely on the mild pictures.

The comparison between the attachment and individuation scores in six areas, mild, strong and total pictures is an essential feature of the test. On the mild pictures the individuation scores should exceed the attachment scores by approximately 40 percent; on the strong pictures the attachment score should exceed the individuation score by approximately the same percentage. On the total pictures the attachment score should generally ex-

ceed the individuation score by 4 to 8 percent. There are of course
many variations within this norm.

As was previously noted, when the individuation responses are
fewer than or equal to the attachment responses on the mild pictures, the interpretation of an anxious attachment disorder may
definitely be posited, especially if the attachment responses on the
mild pictures are many. The severity of the disorder will depend
upon the presence of a low individuation score, a high defensive
pattern, and strong affect reactions. Low individuation scores on
mild as well as total pictures correlate with depressive syndromes,
masochism, and suicidal ideation.

When the percentages of individuation responses are higher than
attachment responses on the strong pictures, a symptom of excessive self-sufficiency appears. Such excessive dependence on self is
often found in individuals with character disorders or psychopathic
problems, or at best in those who tend to overvalue their independence in comparison with their need for others. Their trend is
to create emotional distance from others in order to escape commitments in relationships. Acting out is also a probable interpretation of this pattern, the nature of the actions depending upon the
remainder of the patterns of the protocol. In some youngsters excessive self-sufficiency patterns may have developed as a reaction
formation or defensive maneuver to an unsatisfied symbiotic need,
and instead of having resolved this problem, they had allowed the
"elastic band" to overstretch toward excessive individuation.

In some cases the individuation percentage on the total pictures
is very high but the attachment percentage is within normal limits.
Although this provides evidence of considerable strength in the
personality, it also indicates a degree of excessive self-sufficiency,
but at the same time allowing for closeness. Such persons are
highly motivated toward personal aggrandizement. Reference
will be made to cases in Chapter IV in which both attachment
and individuation scores are strong, as having strong personality
core strength suggesting that such persons have considerable resources in both relationship and self-reliance areas.

Comparisons of attachment ratios and individuation ratios are
referred to as the "attachment-individuation balance." An arith-
metical formulation of this balance was attempted in the original

work on this test. This percentage is described in the protocol form and is obtained according to a method discussed in Hansburg (1972, p. 147, Ref. no. 1). A typical rate is 35 percent. Percentages that drop below 30 should be considered to be in the character disorder range. Those above 45 percent and especially beyond 50 percent must be considered as seriously emotionally disturbed. However, this indicator has some problems, does not work in all cases and should be used only in connection with a careful inspection of each of the figures in the attachment and individuation areas.

A note should be added here with regard to a qualitative difference in the dominant response of the individuation pattern. The sublimation response in this pattern occasionally shows a higher score than adaptation. If this occurs in a high individuation percentage, we are dealing with a much more serious self-sufficiency, avoidance pattern. The same is true if the well-being response dominates the pattern. On the other hand, if such a qualitative difference in the pattern occurs in a low individuation pattern, less significance needs to be attached to this factor. If this qualitative difference occurs in a normal individuation but in a low attachment pattern, we again have evidence of a more seriously disturbed self-sufficiency. If we add to such a qualitative difference a high defensive and possibly a high hostility pattern, severe hostile detachment is posited.

There are numerous variations in the construction of the individuation pattern, especially when one relates the pattern to the attachment pattern. Further, the other patterns to be discussed provide greater understanding of the manner in which individuation is utilized.

Separation Pain Pattern

Emotional pain is the most common accompaniment of trauma, just as physical trauma results in expression of pain. Painful feelings are described as anxiety, fear, and psychosomatic distress. Typically, humans as well as other creatures show emotional pain during separations from familiar persons or surroundings, especially when the separations are sudden, severe, and/or traumatic (see Chapter I). Such normal pain reactions are to be expected on the test. Failure to report such reactions in a reasonable amount is an indication of pathology, just as excessive reactions are also evidence of disorder.

Fewer than 15 percent of the protocol in this area is an indication of separation affect blunting, and more than 17 percent should be considered as strong. Affect blunting in this area usually indicates character malformation; high levels of affect indicate neurotic or sometimes psychotic distress. Most often high levels of pain response are accompanied by high percentages of attachment reactions—a signal of anxious attachment which may or may not be neurotic depending on the remainder of the protocol. When high levels of pain reactions are also contiguous with strong disturbances in the self-evaluative process such as self-love loss, agitated depressive behavior in the face of separation may be expected, especially if the attachment responses are also high.

Occasionally, we find high levels of separation pain in the presence of a low attachment score. A pattern of this nature is likely to be accompanied by a high individuation score. This pattern grouping suggests a more narcissistic concern; that is, the person does not mourn for a lost object but suffers pain because of what will happen to him. Such persons are so involved in gratifying narcissistic needs that they often cannot concentrate on the use of their resources. They are likely to be active, acting-out individuals who are not really comfortable with their own character malformation. The really comfortable character disorder tends to show low levels of separation pain and a constricted picture.

In persons who show low attachment and low individuation percentages, we often find high levels of affect, especially separation pain. In the face of separation or threats of abandonment, such individuals (described as dependent detachment in Chapter I), who have deactivated attachment and individuation systems, show impulsive emotional reactions with very poor control. Nevertheless, despite the high level of affect, their relationships are fundamentally barren and superficial. The prognosis for emotional and social growth is generally poor (see Chapter IV, cases 4 and 5).

The separation pain responses, like many other patterns, are generally fewer on the mild pictures than on the strong pictures. If the responses are equal or if the mild pictures show a predominance of separation pain over the strong pictures, inappropriate affect such as that seen in psychotic disorders may be posited.

Increasing experience with the Separation Anxiety Test Method continues to support the original finding that the fear response dominates this pattern and that generalized anxiety tends to be secondary. Specific fear of an action, a person, a place, or a thing seems to be a strong response to separation experiences, although anxiety often alternates with or substitutes for this response. The two responses run parallel to each other. In disturbed individuals anxiety may well be stronger than the specific fear response.

In cases in which separation pain is high and is dominated by a large number of phobic responses, we are probably dealing with a severe separation phobia. A comparison of these data with the frequency of the "yes" response to the question "Did this ever happen to you?" can determine whether the phobic intensity is related to the actuality of separation trauma. Separation phobias are common in the general population.

On rare occasions we may see a strong dominance of the separation pain pattern by somatic reactions. When this is accompanied by a high attachment level and a low individuation percentage, not only is strong anxious attachment present but it is likely that hysterical psychosomatic phenomena are strong tendencies in this person. We may also find this constellation of responses accompanied by intrapunitive and rejection responses.

In cases in which self-destructive and depressive feelings are involved, affect reactions are usually quite strong, and separation pain contributes greatly to this percentage. These affect reactions will, of course, also include separation hostility as well as excessive reactions to attachment on the mild pictures.

The entire pain system demonstrated by the Separation Anxiety Test Method is a highly sensitive indicator of the alarm threshold. The evidence from varied studies suggests that this pattern, together with the attachment pattern, forms a healthy or disturbed characteristic related to the degree to which separation is felt to be truly alarming. Disturbance in this alarm system indicates the degree to which an individual has departed one way or another from the inherent trends for survival provided by the instinctive need for protection. When these two patterns are low, deactivation has taken place and a disordered approach to separation occurs. When these patterns are excessively high, the individual reacts as though minor separation events are cataclysmic. In either event these patterns provide indications of degrees of past separation traumas.

Separation Hostility Pattern

As previously noted, hostility is a common accompaniment of separation experiences. It is to be expected that degrees of resentment and anger will normally be aroused and demonstrated in the test patterning. When hostility is absent or low, the protocol should be considered as having pathological significance. Obviously the resentments may be felt toward the attachment figure or toward oneself or may be projected outward toward others in the environment. Generally, outright anger dominates the hostility pattern, and the anger is not necessarily of the type that is felt toward anyone. It is simply an expression of a feeling without a specific target. This hostility expression is reported more often than intrapunitive or projection reactions. Normally, the total expression of hostility ranges between 12 and 14 percent of the total number of responses. On the Separation Anxiety Test the percentage of the hostility pattern is generally lower than that of the pain pattern.

The hostility pattern shows a very strong increase from the mild to the strong pictures. This is understandable, because the mild pictures are expected to be low in affect production. The strong separation pictures are of such a nature as to produce strong hostile reactions. If the mild pictures produce nearly as many hostile responses as the strong pictures or if they produce many hostile reactions at all, hostile anxious attachment or hostile detachment is a probable diagnostic conclusion, depending upon the remainder of the protocol. Hostile responses are stronger and more frequent in acting-out individuals than in others.

Recent studies by clinicians demonstrate that when hostility is the dominating pattern of the protocol, dangerous homicidal trends may be inferred. This is a verification of the thesis presented in Volume I Hansburg (1972). Imagined, projected, or even minor separation experience in such cases might easily trigger a severe outbreak of uncontrollable rage. Such rages often lead to destructive, violent acts. The theory previously proposed indicates that deactivation of the attachment pattern reduces controls in those individuals whose attachment experiences in infancy were disappointing and who failed to deal adequately with normal development of aggressiveness.

A dominance of projection as a medium of hostility expression is obviously a paranoid reaction and should be considered as serious, especially on mild pictures. If this pattern is accompanied by a high percentage of individuation responses, we postulate a paranoid personality (see Chapter IV, Case 8). When other factors in the protocol appear to compensate to some degree for the high level of projection responses, a paranoid characteristic to the personality is suggested, even if this does not dominate the individual's reactions to the environment. Again this pattern may be found in both hostile anxious attachment and hostile detachment.

Dominance of the intrapunitive response in the hostility pattern suggests a more masochistic individual. Such a pattern is more likely found in severe anxious attachment. Occasionally it is found in individuals who act out their problems in such a manner as to seek to be punished. Acting out with self-destructive unconscious motivation is a more common type of pathology in adolescence. Hostile anxious attachment cases may include this pattern.

When the total hostility pattern is combined with the total pain pattern and equals a third or more of the responses, we have evidence of strong affect reaction to separation experiences. When this pattern is accompanied by a low attachment level (hostile detachment), the interpretation for this constellation would be a volatile individual with poor controls over emotional reactions during separation experiences, especially when the separation is of considerable import. In cases in which the attachment percentage is below the individuation level and also below normal, and the affect reactions are high, we expect a good deal of acting out during a separation experience or in response to such an experience,

If the percentage of separation hostility reactions is higher than the percentage of separation pain, the interpretation is a circumvention of pain with the expression of reactive anger before the pain is felt (see Chapter IV, Case 6). We would then have to posit impulsive hostility in the person, directed toward either the environment, the self, or both, depending upon which type of response predominates. (See discussion of Hostile Anxious Attachment, Chapter I).

Defensive Process Pattern

As indicated in Volume I Hansburg (1972), a common reaction to separation experiences is an effort to avoid and to deflect the impact of the distress. The author has referred to this as "separation denial" or "reality avoidance," because the ego is not strong enough to absorb the full impact of the separation experience. The problem is dealt with through techniques that save the individual from either severe pain or disorganization. The tactics for these defensive actions as studied by the test consist of withdrawal, disavowal, or fantasy.

Withdrawal from contact may be a short-term or long-term isolation, sometimes just curtailment of verbal or other forms of communication and may have a salutary effect. A complete deflection of the trauma may be achieved by indifference, lack of feeling, not caring, and the like. This facet is referred to as evasion in the test. The third item of this pattern, fantasy, is referred to in the test as a dream of a separation experience rather than a reality. These three responses form a defensive pattern and generally achieve an average percentage between 10 and 13 percent of the total. It is expected that the mild pictures will produce fewer responses in this category than the strong pictures.

The pattern should generally be dominated by the withdrawal response with fantasy, second and evasion, third. The most dominant element in the pattern should be significant. Thus, if evasion is dominant, disorder of the character structure and acting out are more common. When fantasy is more dominant, a safety factor is available which is more therapeutic, more useful in object relations, and more amenable to interactional operations (Hansburg, 1972, no. 1, p. 86).

The acting-out and the delusional types of behavior accompanying separation experiences are often most readily indicated in this pattern. Thus, a very high score, that is, more than 13 percent, indicates a strong defensive posture. If the percentage becomes so

high as to exceed all other percentages, it is a seriously pathological indicator and the nature of the pathology depends upon
which of the three elements indicated above dominate the picture.
High levels of this defensive pattern,when accompanied by high
attachment and low individuation scores as well as by strong
affect, may be interpreted as severe anxious attachment with self-
destructive and depressive behavior likely.

Whenever the defensive pattern is less than 10 percent, there is
more likelihood of a strong reality-oriented individual. Low percentages in this area are more likely to occur in persons with
strong ego formation. Such a pattern is often found in persons
who obtain high percentages on both attachment and individuation patterns. The defensive pattern is more often low in cases of
high individuation and low attachment and is then interpreted as
a further sign of resistance to needfulness. If the attachment level
is high and the individuation is low, a low defensive pattern is an
indication of a poorly defended individual, who is easily exposed
to severe affect, which could be very painful.

High defensive patterns are most commonly seen in many disturbed persons with a variety of diagnostic appraisals. Thus, nine
out of the eleven protocols presented in Chapter IV show defensive pattern percentages of more than 13 percent. In a recent unpublished study* of 25 mothers of five-year-olds, only three
showed such high percentages. In another recent unpublished
study of delinquents, it was found that the records contained high
defense pattern levels. DeLozier (1979) also found very high defense patterns among abusive mothers. It seems likely, therefore,
that this pattern has much diagnostic value in determining the
degree of disturbance. Bowlby (1980) has indicated that the
defensive system, when excessive, is a leading indicator of pathology, and the data from the Separation Anxiety Test appears to
bear out this conclusion.

In the above study of 25 mothers, 17 showed low levels of defensive patterning. In most of these cases greater strength of the
attachment and individuation levels was shown. In a few cases the
low patterns were associated with excessive self-sufficiency and/or
acting out. It can be said that most often low levels are associated
with strength and high levels with disturbance or weakness. A

Study by Hansburg.

reasonable interpretation suggests that pathological formations are bound to develop when too much internal psychic effort flows into the defensive system.

Patterns of the Self-Evaluative System (Self-Love Loss)

Traumatic events in one's life as well as temporary periods of anxiety due to the inaccessibility of a love object tend to produce a lessened sense of the value of the self. The feeling may be expressed as follows: "If I am abandoned or if other people do not want me, then there must be something very unacceptable about me." One can engage in an extensive theoretical discussion as to why a person should experience such a feeling. Why does such a profound sense of not being lovable occur when a person is abandoned by an attachment figure or when a person is threatened with loss of closeness?

When a child or, in fact, a person of any age experiences the loss or threat of loss of a significant attachment figure, the loss of protection is deeply felt (Bowlby, 1969). Once an attachment has been formed with a love object, a prolonged absence from such a person induces the notion that one is not worthy of being wanted or loved. When a child grows up with this feeling and if it becomes an ingrained or egosyntonic characteristic of his personality, he may either spend his life yearning intensely to be loved and wanted or he may react as though it is never possible to be loved and wanted because he is not the kind of person who can be loved and wanted. One of the commonest defenses against this feeling is an addiction of some sort, such as alcoholism, overeating, drug abuse, and related addictions. Individuals who show a strong sense of self-love loss or self-devaluation, especially during separation experiences, have within themselves depressive and self-destructive tendencies.

It is of course possible for youngsters who have never been geographically separated from their parents or overtly rejected to develop such feelings. These feelings may arise from an absence of communication with an attachment figure or from inaccessibility of that figure. In this sense, the separation from a love object is a continuous one, based on a wall of communication failure. Often this communication failure may well be the factor that eventually leads to the child's geographical separation from the parents either voluntarily by running away or by placement. Under these circumstances damage to the entire self-evaluative system is almost inevitable.

The responses of rejection and intrapunitiveness are the two responses in the test which are most representative of the feeling of loss of self-love. These responses are very significant and should be seriously considered in every test protocol. There is some difference between the median responses of the normative populations in self-love loss and those of placed populations of children. The latter is especially true of children who live in cultures where this kind of experience is a common one. Generally speaking, the range of self-love loss responses on the Separation Anxiety Test should be between 5 and 8 percent. More than 8 percent is considered to be strong, and a depressive indicator. If this percentage is greater than the percentage recorded for self-esteem preoccupation (discussed in the following section), it becomes even more significant as a depressive factor and it also has self-destructive implications.

The emphasis in the average case should be on the intrapunitive response rather than on the rejection response. The average individual more readily feels blame for a situation rather than rejection. This result accords well with the rationale involved in the theoretical study of the self-evaluative system. Therefore, the three aspects of this pattern, each of which suggests a depressive tone, include a percentage of more than 8 percent, a higher percentage of self-love loss than self-esteem preoccupation, and an emphasis on rejection rather than on intrapunitiveness.

The pattern described above is a more serious indicator when the individuation percentage is in the weak range and the attachment percentage is strong. It is even more pathological when the attachment percentage on the mild pictures is stronger than the individuation percentage or is equal to it. The indications for severe anxious attachment are then increased when more than one-third of the responses appear in the separation hostility and separation pain patterns. A strong defensive pattern percentage would complete the picture. We can see that the significance of the self-love loss pattern increases considerably when it is associated with other factors in the test protocol.

The proper interpretation of the high percentage in the self-love loss area is that of reactive depression when it occurs without the above factors. In combination with them, however, there is evidence of a more profound depressive problem related to the separation process. In such a case the individual becomes more and more dangerous to himself (Hansburg, 1976). He suffers from a chronic feeling of being unloved and reacts to this feeling with self-deprecation, self-harm, and self-punishment. When hostile anxious attachment is present with a high self-love loss pattern, the reaction to feelings of being unwanted may consist of attacks against others and demands for greater attention and caretaking. These chronic conditions may be likened to Adler's *minder werdikeit's gefiel* (inferiority complex) with the exception that his emphasis on organ deficiency as the basis for this feeling ignores the significance of attachment.

High percentages of self-love loss are rarely associated with a higher individuation than attachment percentage because of the strong correlation between self-love loss and attachment. In cases of this kind, interpretation would suggest an acting-out person with strong self-punishment trends. Case 8 in Chapter IV resembles this type and Case 3 has an aspect of this problem.

We might ask whether the loss of self- love, as indicated in this test, is an egosyntonic or egoalien phenomenon and whether it has occurred at a later stage of development than the early separation-individuation phase. The treatability of this characteristic depends largely on how profound and how early were its manifestations. The Separation Anxiety Test seems to provide some indication of its depth by appraising factors accompanying the self-love loss pattern. Thus, we have a measure of the degree of egoalien characteristic and therefore its treatability.

Since, as has been noted in Chapter I, self-love has its basis in early infantile security with the attachment figure, and is strongly related to this figure's accessibility to infantile signals, separations of varying degrees of connotation may easily induce self-love loss at later stages of development. Bowlby (1973) suggested that even when the early stages are satisfactory, later separation traumas may induce self-love loss. It seems likely that the degree of such feelings indicated by the test and the associated system disturbances in other areas should provide some indication of the most likely period of growth when severe shocks to self-love occurred. Our evidence indicates strong correlation between more serious histories of separation threats and the presence of high degrees of self-love loss. There is also some question as to whether or not some individuals are by nature more vulnerable to loss of self-love during a separation experience, and this factor may be related to an intense need for attachment, which may dominate their personalities (see Chapter I, p. 4).

In constricted records, which are more characteristic of acting-out individuals, self-love loss responses are likely to be less in evidence. By its very nature a constricted record is a form of defensiveness, and therefore feelings of loss of love are more likely to be denied under such circumstances.

Patterns of the Self-Evaluative System
(Self-Esteem Preoccupation)

Originally, in Volume I (Hansburg, 1972), the author had introduced the responses of concentration impairment and sublimation into the test as evidence of concern with thinking and work. To some degree this pattern was a measure of preoccupation with self-esteem. The pattern was contrasted with a self-love loss concern because these two aspects of reaction to separation experiences were considered as somewhat different. This interpretation was based, in part, on White's (1963) theories concerning ego and reality and independent ego energies. The notion was that self-esteem preoccupation represents a later development in the personality than concern with being loved and wanted. Nevertheless, there has always appeared to be, even in this test, a relationship between these two phenomena. It was generally considered that loss of self-love represented a more profound disturbance than the concern with one's thinking powers, or a preoccupation with one's ability to utilize them. Self-esteem grows out of the capacity to use one's powers and to be effective, whereas a feeling of being loved and wanted arises out of the original accessibility of the maternal or surrogate parental figure. Thus, to be wanted and loved is a more profound experience, and to feel confident in one's capacity is more related to being effective in what one does.

Obviously these two characteristics are related. Therefore a comparison between these two sets of figures on the Separation Anxiety Test becomes significant.

It has been our experience with the test that preoccupation with either concentration impairment or sublimation or both generally yields a higher percentage of responses than concern with feelings of rejection and intrapunitiveness. The percentage of responses to the former should run above 8 percent and should generally be higher than the self-love loss percentage. Whenever the percentage of responses in this category becomes excessive, the interpretation may be that the person feels so ineffectual that he must compensate with excessive sublimation or must be obsessed with poor concentration in situations that ordinarily should not require such an attitude. This feeling of being ineffective and lacking in confidence does suggest an overdependence of the ego on an alterego or on a supportive figure whose absence produces the feeling of ineffectuality.

The response of impaired concentration is more frequent on the strong pictures; the sublimation response is more frequent on the mild pictures. Generally, the impaired concentration responses in the total protocol will exceed the sublimation responses. If sublimation assumes too great a role in this percentage and the total percentage in this area is very high, we may infer that too much of the individual's energies are being expended in efforts at competency and effectiveness rather than in efforts at normal emotional outlets or other defenses.

As previously stated, one of the most noteworthy and significant comparisons is the relationship between self-esteem preoccupation and self-love loss during separation experiences. The former should generally include more responses than the latter. When the reverse is true, the individual is subject to depression and to self-destructive tendencies. The theoretical background for this interpretation lies in the fact that feeling loved and wanted depends upon experiences that are somewhat different from feeling effective. Thus, even if we consider Mahler's concept of object constancy (full incorporation of a loving object) as a primary aspect of feeling loved, this may become a prerequisite for feeling competent and effective. Nevertheless, an individual may invest his major efforts in competence and effectance because he is unable to succeed in feeling wanted and cared for. This kind of reaction would most likely be confirmed by other areas of the test protocol.

Separation experiences can be effective in disorganizing the thinking powers of the individual. This problem can often be seen in the behavior of children in school situations in terms of learning difficulties when anxiety is aroused at home by separation disturbances. This is true even when separation disturbances occur in the school setting itself, such as being transferred from one classroom to another, being separated from a close friend after many years of studying together, and similar experiences. The problem is also evident in older people; for example, a person feels in danger of losing a job in which he has been employed for many years. The fact that the ability to organize thinking and to function intellectually is partly dependent upon the relative absence of anxiety is a long-understood concept with regard to human personality. Those individuals who are able to deal effectively with separation experiences may have less need to be preoccupied with their effective thinking powers.

Nevertheless, the preceding problems do not always seem to be true, because in some cases the person handles his problems by constriction and is therefore preoccupied neither with self-love loss nor with self-esteem. People who are relatively unresponsive to environmental stimulation seem to be little concerned with the degree to which they are loved or to which they are effective. They are simply spending time gratifying immediate impulses and other needs. Such characteristics may be seen in the total protocol and are, of course, reflected again in the limited responsiveness to areas such as concentration impairment or sublimation.

Patterns of the Self-Evaluative System (Identity Stress)

In Chapter I reference was made to the sense of identity as a third subsystem of the self-evaluative system. It was stated that the self-love and self-esteem systems finally merge with the social role and that the sense of identity crystallizes. It has been postulated (Hansburg, 1972, no. 1) that when the sense of identity is threatened by separation experiences, the average person soon recovers because he is sufficiently protected by his defenses as well as by self-love and self-esteem. However, since the separation from a close person or a very familiar environment is similar to losing part of the self, it takes some time to recover the sense of identity. The identity stress response on the test gives us some measure of this reaction.

After many years of experience with the identity stress response, we have noted a tendency toward much variation. Low scores are considered to be those below 7 percent, especially between the ages of 11 and 12; beyond that age level, less than 10 percent is considered low. The percentage reaches a peak in mid-adolescence and then begins to drop. In adults the percentage normally runs as low as 4 or 5 percent. More than 9 percent in the younger group and more than 14 percent in the older group (ages 12, 13, 14, and 15) are considered strong. The later drop in this response suggests that separations appear to have less effect in this area in older people, possibly because the sense of identity has already been so well established, whereas in early adolescence it is still in the process of formation.

The interpretation of the frequency of this response has already been discussed to some extent in Chapter II. It was pointed out that very low scores and very high scores have different qualitative interpretations. Individuals with medium scores tend to be most adequate in their maturational judgment.

It is important to note whether the identity stress response is lower or higher on the mild than on the strong pictures. Higher scores on the mild pictures definitely represent poor judgment and lack of adequate differentiation between stimuli, a condition true of other test patterns.

It is obvious that with increasing life experience in dealing with separation, people tend to have less of a feeling of personality change. The test item does not indicate whether the change is positive or negative—but only a feeling of change. In an adolescent this is a common emotional experience as a response to development even though there are good family relationships and there are no real threats of loss or abandonment. Separation feelings occur as a response to growth and are intrapsychic. In adolescents the feelings are often vague stirrings, although sometimes specific with regard to physical and physiological appearances and functioning. In adults, stabilization occurs and only severe crises and threats of abandonment can elicit the identity stress. In the elderly (Hansburg, 1980), illness, bodily deterioration, loss of contact with community, and other factors, create an increasing sense of identity stress, as in adolescents.

The ability to recognize that change occurs in oneself as one experiences separation from significant persons is an essential characteristic of development. It suggests a sense of self, an increasing awareness that one does not remain the same, and an increasing growth potential. Weakness in this area, combined with other patterns, is one of the elements frequently seen in the depressive and self-destructive personality. This is especially true if the trait is associated with low individuation, high emotional level of reactivity, strong attachment levels on mild pictures, high defensive levels, and strong self-love loss.

An excessive responsiveness to the identity stress area in comparison to the rest of the protocol strongly suggests a tendency toward depersonalization and dissociative reactions. The observer should be suspicious of psychotic trends in the face of separation if other factors also appear—for example, an increase in the number of inappropriate or absurd responses as well as high percentages of responses in the defensive system.

Summary of Pattern Interpretations

In the foregoing discussion of pattern interpetations of the Separation Anxiety Test an attempt has been made to indicate some of the major ways in which we may understand the responses to the test. The major variations in the relationships of these patterns have been presented in the hope that the clinician will thereby be able to interpret the results with a maximum of understanding. It is very important that the material in this chapter be related to the theoretical system presented in Chapter I. By so doing meaningful characterizations may be made of children, adolescents, and adults and highly useful clinical evaluations may be obtained.

In the following chapter the full integration of the foregoing material will be presented both in a general way and in specific cases. It is hoped that these intensive examples will further clarify how the test may be utilized in the clinic setting both for purposes of diagnostic evaluation and for therapeutic intervention. The case presentations should also be of assistance in utilizing the test in research programs designed to study separation as a human phenomenon.

IV

INTERPRETATION OF
SEPARATION ANXIETY TEST PROTOCOLS
WITH CLINICAL CASE MATERIAL

In order to integrate all the foregoing material into an evaluation of a Separation Anxiety Test protocol, some case records
have been organized in such a way as to be useful both for clinical
validation of the instrument and for guidance to those who wish
to use the instrument clinically. Each case has been arranged as
follows:

1. Introduction, a statement of what the case illustrates.

2. The Separation Anxiety Test protocol, the individual responses, the pattern analysis, and the evaluation based on the test.

3. The reason(s) for referral.

4. Background material, including case history and events
leading to referral.

5. Psychiatric evaluation.

6. Psychological examination and its interpretation.

7. Validating conclusion.

A variety of cases have been provided in order to illustrate some
of the classifications described as separation disorders in Chapter I,
as well as the various interpretations discussed in Chapters II and
III. Some of these are largely attachment-oriented individuals, some
are mainly individuation-oriented, and others show weakness in
both areas. Further, in one case an entire family was examined
with the test in spite of the absence of validation and reliability

studies on adults (researches in this area are now being successfully conducted—for example, DeLozier, 1979). There is increasing evidence of the validity of the use of the test with entire families, and many such families have already been clinically studied with the instrument (Hansburg, 1975, unpublished study).

Before each case is presented, it is perhaps well to describe how the examiner proceeds to interpret a test protocol and what he looks for. There are so many possible approaches that it would be confusing simply to skip from one response to another and from one picture to another and from one phrase to another. Scores contain a summation of responses to the various categories, such as rejection, impaired concentration, phobic feelings, and others. Furthermore, there are varied responses to each picture, and contradictions in the kinds of responses given to the same picture are apparent. Thus, for example, on the first picture a child may indicate both rejection and fear and at the same time adaptation and sublimation. How can a child have so many different feelings about a separation experience, all at the same time? We must recognize that the makeup of a human being is so complicated that a significant emotional experience can set off a variety of reactions, some of which are contradictory. The same individual, within a few moments of responding to an experience, can waver from one kind of reaction to another, each seeming the exact opposite of the other.

Psychologists' minds are organized in such a way as to constantly search for definity and for concepts that will fit into personality constructs. Where this does not occur, they tend to become confused and disappointed. It is for this reason that the responses to the Separation Anxiety Test have been organized into patterns, which are then provided with dynamic interpretations of intrapsychic interactions and behavioral potential. This assists us in understanding the more dominant movements within the individual and at the same time all the ramified traits and emotional characteristics that ebb and flow at any given time. To apprehend these dominant movements as well as their ramifications is a difficult process in any method of evaluation.

We may begin by examining the number of "yes" and "no" responses to the mental set questions. This will provide a measure of the frequency with which the child has felt separated either emotionally or geographically. We then examine the total number of responses to see whether it fits in with the general averages. In this sense we can determine whether there has been a constricted or an excessive response to the test. Further, we can determine the number of responses to the mild pictures and to the strong pictures and obtain the difference and the percentage this figure is of the total, which should approximate 20 percent. We may then examine the variety of 17 response categories to note quickly where the dominant number of responses lies. This provides some immediate impressions, which may or may not be verified by examining the remainder of the protocol.

Further, we should observe the number of responses to each picture to determine whether any pictures have had an unusual degree of stress or no stress, recognizing that some pictures generally elicit many more responses than others. We may note that some mild pictures have been overstressed, or that there have been underreactions to some strong pictures. This will help to create further impressions. Our attention should also be directed to the number of starred responses—those considered to have a degree of inappropriateness—and whether they are excessive. Thus, by scanning the response chart, we may derive a set of impressions with regard to the youngster, and then elaborate these impressions by more careful study of the patterns.

The most significant patterns are those representing the attachment and individuation (self-reliance) systems. A proper balance between these two patterns on the mild, strong, and total picture summaries is an essential aspect of a healthy adjustment to separation, and this balance gives us a measure of the general strength of the individual during a separation experience. Variations in this balance are possible so long as the major dominance factors are present. Unless we examine very carefully the interrelationships between the mild and strong reactions in both areas, we may be easily misled by the total responses in these areas. Each factor here should be compared with each of the others. Thus, mild attachment should be compared to strong attachment and to mild individuation; mild individuation should be compared to strong individuation and to mild attachment; strong attachment should be compared to strong individuation, and so on. By making these comparisons, a significant understanding of the personality can be achieved. Strengths and weaknesses should be carefully evaluated for possible symbiotic, excessive self-sufficiency, weak core strength, and other characteristics. The nature of this balance is of such importance to the understanding of the Separation Anxiety Test that without it the evaluation of the protocol becomes meaningless.

Once we have seen the trends in the above data, we can proceed to examine the responses to the two major affect areas, separation hostility and separation pain. Proper balance in these affect areas generally consists of a higher level of the latter than of the former; the total percentage of responses to both these areas should be no higher than 30 percent. The affect should be stronger on the strong pictures than on the mild pictures. The emphasis in the hostility area should be on anger, and in the pain area, on fear (phobic). Therefore, with good balance and strength in the attachment and individuation (self-reliance) patterns and with normal percentages of hostility and pain, we will see a personality picture of good potential.

Pathology in the affect area is of definite importance and becomes more highly significant if there are weaknesses anywhere in the attachment and individuation systems. Individuals with characterological disorders inevitably show important imbalances between the affect area and the core attachment-individuation area. Poor balance and high affect are more characteristic of disturbed characters, depending upon whether the imbalance in the attachment-individuation area is due to low attachment response. An imbalanced affect in the presence of high attachment and low individuation is most frequently found in neurotic persons.

The defensive system should then be examined. There should always be a degree of defensive reaction equal to 10 to 13 percent of the total protocol. Whenever this area is too high, it is an indication that the ego feels severely threatened and that the need for avoiding the impact of the separation experience is considerable. It is even more significant of pathology when there has been a drop in the individuation level and when the number of inappropriate responses is above the median. In situations in which the individuation level is high, defensive reactions are excessive and there are many absurd responses, a psychotic acting out can be expected. On the other hand, if the defensive posture is low, it is likely that individuation is high and there is less need for inappropriate reactions. Ordinarily the defensive reaction pattern will be dominated by the withdrawal response, and fantasy responses should be stronger than evasion. If fantasy responses dominate the pattern, while the total defensive system is high, delusional reactions can be expected; if the evasion responses dominate a high defensive pattern, acting out is likely.

A study of the self-evaluative system is then of great assistance. The self-esteem preoccupation level should be stronger than the loss of the loved feeling. When disturbances occur between these two areas, we should again relate them to the attachment-individuation balance, to the degree of affect expressed, and to the defensive system. At the same time we should note the degree of stress on identity, which tells us something of the maturation level or the degree of fragmentation. High levels of responsiveness in the self-evaluative system indicate a definite disorder in the individual's feelings about oneself, and are symptomatic of depressive and self-destructive reactions. Low levels are generally healthier, but still depend upon the major significant factors in the protocol.

Another important element is the percentage difference between the responses to the mild and to the strong pictures. A low percentage is an indication of poor judgment, that is, difficulty in discriminating between the intensity of the stimuli. This suggests a state of confusion and problems of ambivalence, thus resulting in periods of immobilization. A high percentage indicates not only good discrimination but also a state of severe discomfort when mild separation situations give way to strong ones. The degree to which the individual is disrupted by strong separations then becomes excessive.

What emerges from this examination of the Separation Anxiety Test patterned protocol is a dynamic picture of how an individual handles separation experiences and what emotional traits and characteristics have evolved as part of his general personality structure. From this picture we can deduce the degree of health that was achieved in the process of separating from a base of operations, developing exploratory behavior, dealing with affect reactions to separation, handling and controlling the defensive system, developing a self-evaluative system sufficient to feel secure in being wanted, being effective, and finding an acceptable place in the social scheme. It is obvious that the more serious disorders in the character structure are found in those individuals with problems of the attachment-individuation balance.

Caution should be exercised in some cases in which there appears to be rather smooth balances in the attachment and individuation areas but suspicious signs crop up in other areas. This is often noted in individuals who have egosyntonic psychopathic or psychotic conditions with which they are quite comfortable. The disorder usually appears elsewhere in the protocol. Smooth areas of response in such persons are often found in other projective tests, such as the Rorschach inkblots. We should not always expect that the clinical picture derived from this test will provide us with a full diagnostic picture of personality or of emotional disorder, although it often does. What we obtain mainly in this test is a series of patterned reactions and their interaction, which help us to infer what psychological systems and their behavioral correlates are most likely either to dominate separation experiences or to be deactivated. These patterns are highly diagnostic of the dynamic movement within an individual in his relationships with other individuals who are significant persons in his life.

In the accompanying cases the attempt has been made to illustrate the use of the foregoing method in the study of any given youngster or adult. It has been the personal experience of the author as well as of those psychologists who have participated in the use of this instrument that extraordinarily useful and predictive information can be obtained with this test in a clinical setting. This experience has occurred time and again in clinic conferences with social workers and psychiatrists and has resulted in the formulation of plans of a more definitive nature.

The cases selected for presentation consist of youngsters seen at the Jewish Child Care Association, Mt. Sinai Hospital, and Kings County Hospital, all in New York City. It is hoped that these cases will be useful to psychologists in working with the Separation Anxiety Test.

CASE 1: P.G., Male, aged 17½

An adolescent who suffers from severe anxious attachment with overwhelming separation anxiety, is unable to utilize his personal resources in dealing with his environment, and is subject to feelings of unreality and self-denigration.

Introduction

This case is an example of an attachment-oriented individual with deep symbiotic needs, whose individuation system has been deactivated by his severe anxious attachment. This youngster has severe phobias and anxieties when faced with even minor separations from parental attachment figures or other significant figures for whom he has developed an attachment. Further, the case illustrates the effort to deny separation through magical or delusional thinking and poor reality testing. Since the dominant affect in this type of case is represented by specific fears and general distress, we may expect severe disturbance in relation to school or work attendance, inability to travel, and other areas.

On the basis of the Separation Anxiety Test this type of severe disability is associated with vulnerability to self-destructiveness, resulting from the youngster's fear of facing inevitable separation from attachment figures. From a theoretical point of view it is likely that the disorder is related to the crucial period of what Mahler (1968) has referred to as the separation-individuation process at a time when the child's greatest concern about maternal availability reached the highest stage of ambivalence.

The case further illustrates how in adolescence difficulties are intensified because this stage of development increases the psychological and geographical demands for separation from attachment figures for longer periods and for the more adequate establishment of new attachments. In such cases as the present one concentration impairment is another significant characteristic of the disturbance. The youngster is so overwhelmed by the affect engendered by separation that his powers of thinking become disorganized.

Separation Anxiety Test Results

This adolescent was seen at Mt. Sinai Hospital by Dr. Nucia Shimrat, psychologist. On the Separation Anxiety Test, P.G. gave 101 responses (see Chart for Controlled Association Responses). This is nearly twice the number of responses given by adolescents, an obsessive reaction generally referable to intensive internal ambivalence. The largest number of responses given to any picture was 11 and this number was also produced by the class transfer picture, which is in the mild category. Such a large number of responses to a relatively mild stimulus indicates an excessive and pathological reaction and appears specifically related to the school situation. The class transfer picture seemed to elicit a similar intensity of reaction, as the death of the mother picture, a serious sign of disturbance. Noteworthy were the 7 similar responses which were given to both pictures. Yet on the mental set questions the subject reported experiencing only 5 of the 12 separations depicted, and these were all on the mild pictures. The realities of his actual separations therefore did not accord with the intensity of his distress.

There were 47 responses to the mild pictures and 54 responses to the strong pictures, a difference of 9 and a differential percentage of 8. Since 20 percent is the average, this percentage of 8 would be considered very low and an indication of an impairment of judgment in relation to separation stimuli. We have to interpret this factor as a high degree of ready sensitivity to any minor separation and an intense readiness to alarm.

As noted in the chart the most frequent reactions were anxiety, loneliness, somatic reaction, and anger, and, as will be seen later, represented strong affect reaction to separation. The excess of somatic reactions suggested an intense concern with bodily pain in states of alarm by even mild separation experiences, a serious pathological problem.

The pattern of the Separation Anxiety Test (see Pattern Summary Chart) revealed five factors of a severe anxious attachment disorder described in Chapter I (p. 16). An examination of the balance of attachment and individuation (self-reliance) responses on the *mild* pictures indicated a higher score in the attachment area, a pathognomic symbiotic indicator. At the same time the individuation percentage was extremely low in the total score for all pictures. The young man showed a weakness of coping mechanisms for separation situations. The general disturbance in the attachment individuation balance was therefore very clear. Specifically, there were 8 attachment responses on the mild pictures and only 6 individuation responses, a strong reversal of the norm. At the same time there were only 2 individuation responses on the strong pictures and 12 responses of attachment on these pictures, a very significant difference. With a total percentage of 20 in attachment and only 8 in individuation, the above conclusion of serious coping weakness were demonstrated.

The meaning of the above pattern lies in its evidence to severe weakness in exploratory behavioral reactions and the need to maintain proximity to an attachment figure or whatever symbols represent the attachment figure. At this stage of life such weakness can have devastating effects on the functioning capacity to deal with minor daily separations that come within the experience of typical persons.

The affect system was also severely disturbed, with 43 percent of the responses in the fear-anxiety-pain system and in the hostility system, with the most serious disturbance in the former. The fear-anxiety-pain system showed the largest number of responses, 29 percent, of the total protocol. This was far in excess of what would ordinarily be expected and was also considerably above the attachment level. The obvious overwhelming affect reaction to even minor separation pictures was considered to be an extreme sensitivity. This marked affect reaction is a common sign in severe anxious attachment and is often accompanied by symbiotic desires. Further, such overwhelming affect must have a disorganizing effect on ego functioning, both intrapsychically and behaviorally.

P.G. CHART FOR CONTROLLED ASSOCIATION RESPONSES

Picture Number	I	II	III	IV	V	VI	VII	VIII	IX	X	XI	XII	Total	Mild	Strong
Mental Set Response	N	Y	Y	Y	Y	N	N	Y	Y	N	N	Y	5	5	0
Separation Intensity	S	M	M	M	M	S	M	S	M	S	S	S			
Rejection	2	8	(15)	4*	(13)	10*	14*	11	15	(11)*	(6)	(5)	5	2	3
Impaired Concentration	(17)	(11)	11	(1)	(6)	(4)	(11)	15	16	(17)	(16)	(15)	9	4	5
Phobic Feeling	8	(2)	(9)	(3)	(3)	(3)	(4)	(6)	2	15	(8)	(11)	9	5	4
Anxiety	(9)*	(16)	(1)	(2)	(11)	(5)	13	(12)	12*	(9)	(2)	(10)	10	4	6
Loneliness	(5)	15	(5)	(16)	(17)	(9)	(6)	(16)	17	(16)	(15)	(17)	10	4	6
Withdrawal	(3)	12	8	(13)	7	12	8	(7)	(3)	4	9	14	4	2	2
Somatic	4	(14)	(2)	(10)	(2)	(11)	(15)	(8)	14	(7)	(13)	(7)	10	5	5
Adaptive Reaction	(7)	(7)	(13)	14	14	15	12	4	(10)	(8)	11	8	5	3	2
Anger	(11)	(13)	14	(6)	(2)	(1)	(5)	(14)	1	(1)	(5)	(2)	10	4	6
Projection	10	17	3*	17*	(8)	6	9*	(1)	6	14	(10)	6	3	1	2
Empathy	16	(3)*	(12)	9*	1*	(13)	1	(5)	13*	10	(14)	12*	5	2	3
Evasion	6	1	6	5*	10	14	(16)	(9)	4	5	7	4	2	1	1
Fantasy	(14)	10	(7)	(15)*	5*	(17)	3	(2)	9	(6)	(12)	(9)	8	2	6
Well-Being	1	(9)	4	8	16	2	17	10*	(7)	3	4	1	2	2	0
Sublimation	15*	(5)	16	7	9	7	10	13	11	12	17*	13	1	1	0
Intrapunitive	13	(4)	17	12*	15	16*	2*	3*	8	13	3*	3	1	1	0
Identity Stress	(12)	(6)	(10)	(11)	4	8	(7)	17	5*	(2)	(1)	16	7	4	3
TOTAL	8	11	9	9	8	8	7	10	3	9	11	8	101	47	54

72

P.G.
PATTERN SUMMARY CHART

RESPONSE PATTERN	Number of Responses		Total	% of Total Protocol	Area of Emphasis	Comment
	Mild II, III, IV, V, VII, IX	Strong I, VI, VIII, X, XI, XII				
Attachment (Sum of rejection, loneliness, and empathy)	8	12	20	20%	Loneliness	Too strong on mild pictures.
Individuation (Sum of adaptation, well-being, and sublimation)	6	2	8	8%	Adaptation	Too weak
Hostility (Sum of anger, projection and intrapunitiveness)	6	8	14	14%	Anger	Norm but too strong on mild pictures
Painful Tension (Sum of phobic, anxiety, and somatic reactions)	14	15	29	29%	Anxiety and Somatic	Abnormally high
Reality Avoidance (Sum of withdrawal, evasion, and fantasy)	5	9	14	14%	Fantasy	Strong and abnormal emphasis
Concentration Impairment and sublimation (Self-esteem preoccupation)	4:1	5:0	9:1	10%	Concentration impairment	Norm but emphasis excessive
Self-love Loss (Sum of rejection and intrapunitiveness)	3	3	6	6%	Rejection	Norm
Identity Stress	4	3	7	7%	–	Weak
Absurd Responses	2	2	4	–	–	Borderline
Attachment-Individuation Balance	–	–	28	28%	–	Weak
Mild-Strong Scores & %	Score 47 46%	Score 54 54%	Diff. 9	Diff. 8%	–	Weak

Along with this affect disturbance, there was an elevated percentage of 14 percent in the defensive system, and the emphasis was on the fantasy response rather than on withdrawal. This suggested that the defensive system had taken on a delusional aspect and introduced magical thinking. Under such circumstances it seemed that separation experiences for P.G. were so devastating as to overwhelm and distort the defensive system, thus producing psychotic thinking and behavior. This was demonstrated further by the slight elevation in the number of inappropriate or absurd responses (four instead of two or three). This factor usually indicates a tenuous hold on reality.

What effect was shown on his self-evaluative system? Noticeable weaknesses were indicated in self-love and in the capacity to handle identity stress, as demonstrated by the large number of rejection responses. Further, impairment of concentration was quite extensive. Strong interference with intellectual functioning therefore was likely to occur. The evidence further indicated great difficulty in dealing with fundamental instinctual wishes for fear of personality disintegration. Although in adolescence there is usually a capacity to accept identity stress in order to move toward maturity, this was obviously a problem in P.G.'s case.

In summary, the Separation Anxiety Test clearly demonstrated the severe anxious attachment present in this case. Feelings of separation were extremely rampant even on the mild pictures indicating severe separation anxiety and somatic pain, a strong stimulation toward symbiotic need, severe coping distress, limitations in normal exploratory behavior, an invasion of thinking powers with a tenuous hold on reality, and a delusional defensive pattern. The youth's self-evaluative system underwent continuous undermining as a result of his preoccupation with separation, with an attendant difficulty in gratifying normal instinctual urges. There was no doubt that deactivation of several important psychological systems had occurred and had left the youth highly vulnerable to the slightest evidence of separation stress.

Referral Problem

P.G. was hospitalized at Mt. Sinai Hospital for a time and was sent home. His chief complaint was severe anxiety, and he considered hospitalization as an adjustment of medication, which his private psychiatrist had recommended. The patient dated his illness to two years prior to placement, when his parents, who were both schoolteachers, decided to return to work at a camp for the summer. Although this had been their custom for many years, they had not done so for three years prior to this time. P.G. was very upset about his return to camp, became very anxious, began to miss school and developed such symptoms as headaches, dizziness, and chest pains. The parents did visit him and with this assurance he was able to tolerate his camp stay for three weeks, after which he returned to his home and stayed alone for one month. Visits to many medical internists did not produce any physical evidence of the origin for his somatic complaints. He was then referred to a psychiatrist, with whom he began treatment.

He visited the psychiatrist for treatment once and sometimes twice a week. Because he had become more dependent upon his mother in the preceding two years, he became anxious when she was not around. He had been on 800 milligrams of Thorazine per day during the summer in which he was supposed to be in camp, but this medication was discontinued because he developed a disturbance in blood chemistry. Most recently he had been placed on 200 milligrams of Melaril per day and on 5 milligrams of Valium three times a day. However, despite psychiatric and psychopharmacological treatment, he continued to have very severe anxiety attacks.

The summer prior to his admission to the hospital, the patient went with his parents to the New Jersey shore, where the anxiety attacks became more acute. According to his psychiatrist, P.G. was suffering from severe attacks, which included depersonalization and derealization. He had always been regarded as generally phobic, but his phobias had become more severe and he was unable to tolerate being in trains, department stores, or anywhere other than his own home. He had not attended school for about a month prior to admission, and he had been recommended to the hospital for evaluation and adjustment of his medication.

Background Information

P.G. was the middle of three children, born and raised in New Jersey. His older brother, aged 24, was in a medical school training program; his younger sister, aged 8, was attending a public school. At age 4 she had been sent to a psychiatrist for one year for encopresis. P.G. was the product of a normal pregnancy and a normal delivery and apparently showed normal developmental milestones. It was possible that the reports of development overlooked some significant traumas, which either had gone unnoticed or were ·deliberately glossed over. According to the parental statements, his emotional disturbance began to manifest itself at the age of 8 or 9, soon after the birth of his sister. He developed ritualistic behavior at night, which included touching the wall, touching things in the closet, and looking under his bed. He was taken to a psychologist for examination and then to a psychiatrist, who recommended that the father spend more time with P.G. The father had been working at several jobs for financial reasons and had limited time for his family. After nine months, psychotherapy was discontinued because there was no improvement.

P.G. had achieved average grades in elementary school and an 83·percent average in high school, thus indicating reasonably good academic success. He had no apparent peer relationship problems until two years prior to hospital admission, when he began to isolate himself from close relationships with his peers. He derived his greatest comfort from his home, where he spent most of his time. In high school he had won several science awards, the most recent one having been for the creation of equipment producing his own laser beam. During his socialization period, he had dated girls on a few occasions, but had no such contacts during the year prior to this referral.

These bare facts of the background history provided very little understanding of the dynamics responsible for P.G.'s disturbance. However, the data do indicate that from very early childhood P.G. was highly vulnerable to disturbance, especially phobic and compulsive behavior. The fact that the mother returned to work when P.G. was 3 years old is not necessarily in and of itself an indication of an unobserved or unreported separation disturbance, but it appears quite likely that he never really adequately accepted the separation. Since the most obvious disturbance developed when his sister was born and when he was separated from his mother for a period, it appeared likely that he was no longer able to defend himself against the internal distress that had gone relatively unnoted earlier.

Psychiatric Interview

The psychiatrist reported that P.G. was a good-looking young man, much younger looking than his stated age and dressed casually but very conservatively. He related in a somewhat distant manner but was cooperative. He seemed guarded and evasive, stating that he did not remember too many answers to questions and asked the psychiatrist to request his record from his previous therapist. He spoke in a clear, soft voice; his thought content centered around his anxiety in general and about his stay in the hospital in particular. He expressed a major concern about his medication, especially that he was not able to obtain medication when he desired it. He revealed no obvious thought disorder, no loosening of associations, and no circumstantiality. His proverb interpretations were concrete, and he appeared unable to abstract from many of them. He denied having hallucinations or delusions, although he reported hearing his own thoughts and described periods of derealization and depersonalization. He was oriented in time and could attend to numbers spoken backward and forward. He demonstrated poor judgment in his response to a number of questions, and his mood was anxious and slightly depressed. It was also evident that his physical health had been somewhat impaired. The psychiatrist was most impressed with the phobic elements in the boy's personality. After some adjustment of medication, P.G. was discharged from the hospital and sent home.

Psychological Examination

The psychologist agreed that P.G. looked younger than his years, that his behavior was very passive and somewhat depressed, and that the most striking feature was the blandness of his affect. The young man attributed his anxiety disturbance to the separation from his parents but was unable to elaborate on the statement or to describe what he meant, except to say that he felt dizzy and anxious.

Intellectually, he measured in the high average-to-bright normal range, Wechsler Intelligence full scale I.Q 112. There were no indications of any higher potential. This would hardly be ideal for the exacting standards and expectations of his family, especially in view of the older brother's high academic success. Strivings for achievement were inferred from his highest score on the arithmetic subtest, which the psychologist reported did not reflect better capabilities, but rather signified that P.G. was probably an overachiever who was making a great effort to conform—a pattern seen in one of his stories in the thematic apperception test.

The psychologist reported that when P.G. was asked about his siblings, he talked about his sister but never mentioned his brother. Such an oversight was not considered to be accidental, thus suggesting considerable defensive exclusion in relation to his brother and to his position in the family constellation. Generally, P.G. seemed to communicate in a tangential manner, unable to attack a problem directly. He presented contradictions in thinking that reflected his ambivalance about his human contacts and his withdrawal from them. His greatest fear was expressed in the following words: "being alone with nobody else." Yet, despite this fear of being alone, he expressed a desire to go to the moon some day. The evidence suggested that he tended to withdraw from interpersonal contacts into an apparent regressed and isolated state and yet was afraid to be alone because of his threatening fantasies.

The psychologist averred further that P.G. was "childish and immature" and that his "ego regression" probably dated back to the age of 6, when he had had an ear operation (unreported above) prior to the birth of his sister. This condition was suggested by drawings of his family, which consisted of parents and a boy of 6. Furthermore, his problems reportedly began at age 8 or 9, subsequent to his sister's birth. It seemed that before the birth of his sister he had received more attention and had resented forfeiting it after her birth. An example of this interpretation made by the psychologist was P.G.'s identification with a dog on one of the tests, because, as he said, "dogs get a lot of attention." Another interpretation of the tests indicated that he appeared irritated by his sister because she pestered him a great deal. In his family drawing the mother's arms were in front of her body and both parents had empty, unseeing eyes, thus implying that they did not pay attention to him and were unavailable for his need satisfactions. On the basis of this material the psychologist stated that the data showed strong obsessive-compulsive features with intellectualization, rationalization, and isolation of affect.

Results of the Rorschach test showed marked phobic and paranoid elements in the boy's personality. None of his defenses were working for him. The phobic component accelerated his withdrawal and P.G. projected his oral-aggressive impulses onto the environment, perceiving "claws," "fangs," "spiders," and "insects." The psychologist made the usual intepretation of the paternal image (Card IV)—"a giant insect," whose claws, feet, and mouth were ready to jump on whatever it caught—a dangerous and unknown force that could destroy him. The maternal image, on the other hand, brought out intellectualized and amorphous responses, underscoring the lack of warmth or positive feeling for him.

Further interpretations suggested that despite his isolation, P.G. felt that he had sufficient inner resources to function autonomously. Yet he had no sense of self, no core, and felt empty and lacking in substance, just like his percept of an "amoeba" and the numerous "skeletons" on the Rorschach test. He felt the need for the constant presence of his parents and lacked confidence in his ability to lead an independent life. Many of his TAT stories indicated that he would be unassertive on a job, completely dependent upon his parents, and unable to survive on his own. Using typical psychosexual terminology, the psychologist suggested that P.G. would undoubtedly continue to be overcome by extreme threats of castration and would remain conforming and submissive. The major emphasis in the stories revolved around passivity coupled with feelings of complete helplessness and no resources to manage in a stressful situation. Events were seen as generally not within his control even when choices of actions were available to him. It was also interesting that many of his stories referred to the adult males in the pictures as "boys." The psychologist suggested that this was a defense against some problems in his relationship with his father, reflecting his need to deny threatening masculine aggression, which he attempted to deal with by projecting it on to boys.

The psychologist's impression was that P.G. was going through the motions of making an adaptation but was not successful; the result was total hopelessness and helplessness, with apathy and a deep feeling of resignation. There were two clearly suicidal stories, one with inappropriate affect and the other in reaction to the loss of a spouse. In the second story, suicide was committed not on impulse but in a premeditated manner, which, diagnostically, was even more serious. P.G.'s reality testing was seen as undermined and with evidence of a gross thought disorder. His verbal facade was described as very precarious. The psychologist offered the diagnostic impression of a decompensating obsessive-compulsive adolescent with a schizophrenic core, phobic and paranoid. Prognosis was considered to be guarded because of the extreme withdrawal and paucity of inner resources.

Validating Conclusion

It is not at all remarkable that a test method like the Separation Anxiety Test would present such a valid evaluation of a case of this kind, because it was well designed for such problems. In fact, it could be said that the problems of diagnosis, therapy, and prognosis in cases of this kind do not require any brilliant analytical judgment. The disturbance was clearly evident in the referral and the background material. Nevertheless, the purpose of using the Separation Anxiety Test in this case was to determine how well it would bring out the nature of the disturbance.

Although on the one hand the language of the test is different in a number of respects from that used by either the psychiatrist or the psychologist who examined the boy, many areas of agreement were highly correlative. In the test the term "severe anxious attachment" was used as a diagnostic category; the psychiatrist referred to the boy as phobic and the psychologist produced an elaborate statement of "decompensating obsessive-compulsive adolescent with a schizophrenic core, phobic and paranoid." In the test, reference was made to the poor resource level (individuation); the same references were made by the psychologist but in a different context. The test suggested a delusional defensive system and tenuous reality testing; the psychologist referred to this as a breakdown in the defensive system. The test indicated a breakdown in thinking capacity; the psychologist used the term "thought disorder." These examples indicate the difference in language, despite much agreement in essential aspects.

The test was an essential corroboration that P.G. had suffered from a separation disturbance for much of his life, but in addition used the term symbiotic to refer to the boy's intense attachment need. It suggested that there were actual symbolic forms of separation—for example, the ear operation at age 6; the birth of the sister; going to camp with his parents, all of which meant leaving home. It was obvious from the test that this boy had adopted a variety of defenses which did not work and that he was a highly vulnerable and sensitive personality. The self-destructive elements revealed in the test were corroborated by several TAT stories, but in the Separation Anxiety Test it was possible to obtain a definitive and objective measure of this self-destructive phenomenon. Further, and what is most important, this boy's perception of his parents, as revealed by the psychologist's examination, was not without foundation in reality as revealed by the Separation Anxiety Test. Although he received protection, he obviously was never adequately provided with the necessary basic caretaking that would have provided the strength needed for the self-evaluative system.

Even though the prognosis in the psychological examination was guarded, the Separation Anxiety Test strongly suggested that with long-term dedicated treatment this boy could be helped considerably. He showed adequate attachment need and strong affect—all of which indicated that the boy could form a relationship which would make growth possible; because it was highly doubtful that he could improve spontaneously, psychotherapy was considered to be the major treatment of choice. Furthermore, whereas efforts should be directed to the reduction of the intensity of his fears and anxieties, treatment would eventually have to be extended to the intense symbiotic condition, which is at the root of his disorder. Prognosis in cases of this kind is often called guarded, simply because the patient needs a therapist who is dedicated and accessible—and such a person is difficult to find.

CASE 2   E.F. Female, aged 14½

*An adolescent girl with strong anxious attachment,
with an underlying symbiotic problem, but with
adequate resources to deal with her environment.
She is unable to gratify her strong attachment
needs, although she has adequate reality testing but
she is nevertheless suffering from a degree of separation anxiety.*

Introduction

This case is an illustration of strong anxious attachment with an
underlying symbiotic problem in which strong attachment need
remains unsatisfied, although an adequate individuation system
is available for personal development. While a sufficiently strong
affect is present as a result of separating experiences, it is not so
intense as in Case 1. There is no doubt, however, that a great degree of separation anxiety is present.

As in the first case, we do see strong separation defensiveness,
which may move this girl in a direction similar to that in the first
case, except that reality testing is far better than in the preceding
case. Nevertheless, one would expect this girl to shy away from
contact with others because of her need for fantasy. Some youngsters are able to avoid losses of reality by using other defenses,
such as adequate fantasy levels without magical thinking. Another
significant factor illustrated by this case is psychosexual immaturity, which was seen in all investigations of this girl, in addition
to the Separation Anxiety Test.

The self-evaluative system is also suffering from some damage in
this case and could result in depressive manifestations. This is a
common occurrence when the mother dies, even when the death
occurs during the latency period. It illustrates what happens when
an anxiously attached child experiences the death of the mother
and then life afterward with a surrogate figure. It seems that an
anxiously attached child has great difficulty in becoming attached
to a surrogate figure, and remains psychologically loyal to the dead
maternal figure. The unresolved loneliness and difficulty in forming
new relationships can lead to unhappy consequences.

Separation Anxiety Test Results

On the Separation Anxiety Test E.F. gave 65 responses, 22 on the mild pictures and 43 on the strong pictures. Whereas the total responsiveness is within the norm, her responses to the strong pictures were far more intense than would be expected when they are related to the mild pictures. The difference is 33 percent, which is quite high, thus indicating that ordinarily mild separations would not be disturbing but she would overreact to strong stimuli. The dominant reactions on the mild pictures were in the loneliness and adaptive areas, with additional responsiveness in the fear and withdrawal areas. On the more intense separation pictures, empathy dominated the scene and was followed by clusters of responses in the adaptive, withdrawal, and fear areas. As one might have suspected, the child showed the largest number of responses (11) to the maternal death picture; the hospitalization-of-the-mother and the argument-between-the-mother-and-the-father pictures each produced 7 responses.

Reference to the Pattern Summary Chart shows that the largest percentage of responses was given in the attachment area (23 percent). The symbiotic problem was demonstrated by the fact that there are 5 attachment and 5 individuation responses on the mild pictures (see Chapter I, p. 16). Primarily more individuation responses would be expected on these pictures than attachment responses. Further evidence of the symbiotic problem was shown by the almost equal number of responses to individuation on both the mild and strong pictures. This pattern provided evidence of a sensitive individual, strongly attached to a maternal figure.

The second strongest pattern was in the area of the defensive system (20 percent). This represented a defensive production far higher than is found in the general population. There was a total of 7 withdrawal and 5 fantasy responses. The potential for a delusional type of reaction was present and there was a definite suggestion that the failure to deal adequately with the loss of the mother had been responsible for this reaction. This pattern projected the possibility that E.F. was likely to be a loner who was dissatisfied with her status but who was unable to deal with it. Feelings of loneliness and a considerable amount of anxiety then followed.

E.F. CHART FOR CONTROLLED ASSOCIATION RESPONSES

Picture Number	I	II	III	IV	V	VI	VII	VIII	IX	X	XI	XII	Total	Mild	Strong
Mental Set Response	NY	NY	YY	Y	YYY	NN	NY	NY	N	YY	YY	NYY	5	3	2
Separation Intensity	S	M	M	M	M	S	M	S	M	S	S	S			
Rejection	2	8	15	4*	13	10*	14*	11	15	11*	(6)	(5)	2	0	2
Impaired Concentration	17	11	11	1	(6)	(4)	(11)	15	16	(17)	(16)	15	5	2	3
Phobic Feeling	8	(2)	9	(3)	3	(3)	4	(6)	(2)	(15)	(8)	11	7	3	4
Anxiety	9*	16	(1)	2	(11)	(5)	13	12	12*	(9)	(2)	10	5	2	3
Loneliness	(5)	(15)	(5)	16	17	(9)	(6)	16	(17)	16	(15)	17	7	4	3
Withdrawal	(3)	12	(8)	13	(7)	(12)	(8)	7	3	4	(9)	(14)	7	3	4
Somatic	4	14	2	10	12	11	15	8	14	7	13	7	0	0	0
Adaptive Reaction	(7)	(7)	(13)	14	(14)	15	12	(4)	(10)	(8)	(11)	8	8	4	4
Anger	(11)	13	14	(6)	2	(1)	5	14	1	1	5	(2)	4	1	3
Projection	10	17	3*	17*	8	6	9*	1	6	14	10	6	0	0	0
Empathy	(16)	3*	12	9*	1*	(13)	1	(5)	13*	(10)	(14)	(12*)	6	0	6
Evasion	6	1	6	5*	10	14	16	9	4	5	7	(4)	1	0	1
Fantasy	14	(10)	(7)	15*	5*	17	3	(2)	9	(6)	(12)	9	5	2	3
Well-Being	(1)	9	4	8	16	2	17	(10*)	7	3	4	1	2	0	2
Sublimation	15*	5	16	(7)	9	7	10	13	11	12	17*	13	1	1	0
Intrapunitive	13	4	17	12*	15	16*	2*	3*	8	13	(3*)	(3)	2	0	2
Identity Stress	12	6	10	11	4	8	7	(17)	5*	(2)	(1)	16	3	0	3
TOTAL	6	4	5	3	4	7	3	6	3	7	11	6	65	22	43

E.F.

PATTERN SUMMARY CHART

RESPONSE PATTERN	Number of Responses		Total	% of Total Protocol	Area of Emphasis	Comment
	Mild II, III, IV, V, VII, IX	Strong I, VI, VIII, X, XI, XII				
Attachment (Sum of rejection, loneliness, and empathy)	5	10	15	23%	Loneliness	Norm
Individuation (Sum of adaptation, well-being, and sublimation)	5	6	11	17%	Adaptation	Norm
Hostility (Sum of anger, projection and intrapunitiveness)	1	5	6	9%	Anger	Low but emphasis normal
Painful Tension (Sum of phobic, anxiety, and somatic reactions)	5	7	12	18%	Phobic	Strong Emphasis normal
Reality Avoidance (Sum of withdrawal, evasion, and fantasy)	5	8	13	20%	Withdrawal	Very strong Emphasis normal
Concentration Impairment and sublimation (Self-esteem preoccupation)	2:1	3:0	5:1	9%	Concentration impairment	Norm but Emphasis strong
Self-love Loss (Sum of rejection and intrapunitiveness)	0	4	4	6%	None	Norm
Identity Stress	0	3	3	5%	–	Weak
Absurd Responses	0	3	3	–	–	Norm
Attachment-Individuation Balance	–	–	12	18%	–	Weak
Mild-Strong Scores & %	Score 22 34%	Score 43 67%	Diff. 21	Diff. 33%	–	Very High

85

It is significant that the fear-anxiety-pain system was strong (18 percent), but not strong enough to deal with the girl's powerful defensive system. In order to allay the feeling of loneliness, the pain system should usually be strong enough to drive the youngster into seeking relationships. In this case this system did not operate too well and the defensive system took over, with the resultant tendency to withdraw and to fantasize rather than to relate. Therefore, one significant technique E.F. adopted in the face of separations was an internal effort to alleviate, instead of an environmental, behavioral one. This is not to say that acting out may not occasionally be employed in such situations, but rather that the former tactic was more prevalent than the latter.

In this case the hostility system dropped below the norms and far below the fear-anxiety-pain system. This demonstrated further that we were dealing with a strong anxious attachment instead of a hostile anxious attachment. If hostility is manifested, it would have been provoked by environmental factors rather than by internal need. These external forces were often represented by the behavior of individuals with whom the subject was living or with whom she was required to relate against her will.

The self-evaluative system seemed to have been most affected in the identity stress area. This reaction, although often associated with immaturity in the psychosexual development, also indicated a loss of E.F.'s sense of personal role in the social milieu. Fear of handling instinctual needs became a critical problem.

According to the Separation Anxiety Test protocol some aspects of the self-evaluative system appeared to be relatively intact. Concentration impairment, however, seemed to be a problem, a factor that suggested some loss of confidence in relation to thinking powers. In view of the fact that self-love loss was not dominated by rejection, it is likely that the basic feeling of being a loved person is not particularly damaged.

The emphasis in the test had, therefore, been largely on the symbiotic problem, the strong separation pain system, and the severe separation defensiveness in a person with adequate individuation resources. The patterns of the test strongly suggested the need for, and the capacity to profit from, psychotherapy. As will be seen later, this recommendation was made by other staff workers as well. While some depressive reactions could occur, they would not be the most dominant ones in E.F.'s future or potential personality makeup.

Referral Problem

E.F. was referred to the Jewish Child Care Association by her father and her stepmother, because they considered her to be difficult, negative, provocative, unable to get along with anyone in the family, and without friends. In addition to these problems, it was understood from the social worker's interview that E.F.'s identity as a boy or a girl had frequently been questioned by other children. The stepmother was greatly concerned that E.F. might harm her younger stepsisters. It was also reported by the parents that E.F. desired to live away from home because she could not bear to live with her stepmother and was very unhappy with her stepsisters.

Background Information

E.F. was one of six children living with the father and stepmother. Two of the children were stepsisters, children of the stepmother, and were younger than E.F. Her own two older brothers and older sister were attending high school and college. The older sister had been living away from home while attending college.

E.F. was very close to her mother, who died when E.F. was 8 years old. Any discussion of the mother by the social worker brought tears to E.F.'s eyes. A cat E.F. had been fond of and which lived with the family while E.F.'s mother was alive disappeared after it had died, and the family suspected that E.F. had buried the body herself. The natural mother was a warm, maternal, outgoing, and very active woman, who stayed at home until E.F. was 6 and in the first grade in school. At that time the mother became employed outside the home. E.F. then transferred her intense attachment from her mother to her older sister, who later took care of her after the mother had died. The older sister was very stern and often struck E.F.

E.F. began to menstruate at age 11 but tended to avoid identification with women, wearing baggy slacks and loose-fitting turtleneck sweaters in a more exaggerated form than acceptable in the cultural setting. E.F. was overweight because she had fits of overeating. Except for such periods of overindulgence in food, the history was that of a child with essential normal development. Her figure was reported to be childish, although her breasts had just begun to develop.

E.F. had done well in school and maintained a high average, despite her other difficulties. The stepmother was inclined to feel that the higher marks in school were based on the sympathetic attitude of the teachers rather than on valid performance. Behaviorally the school reported that E.F. was a loner and often lied to her teachers but the specific lies were not reported. It was further indicated by the school that she initially evoked a warm response from adults but that this impression did not last. Both parents were in strong agreement about placement for E.F. They resisted attempts at private psychotherapy for her, and did not want to participate in family therapy in a psychologist's office. The parents felt that they could not continue to live with her during a period of therapy.

E.F. reported that she did not like her parents and wanted to live away from them, preferably with a maternal aunt and uncle, but apparently this arrangement was not possible. It was the social worker's impression that E.F. would be better off at home under treatment, but the parents' insensitivity and rejection convinced the worker that E.F. should be placed. The worker interpreted that E.F. was still bereaved over the mother's death and had been unable to accept the stepmother as a surrogate because the stepmother lacked warmth. It was apparent that the girl felt isolated in her home, especially after her sister had left for college and the favored aunt and uncle had moved away.

Psychiatric Interview

The psychiatrist observed that E.F. was a short, chubby, and unattractive adolescent who looked her stated age of 14½. When first seen in the waiting room, it was impossible to determine her sex because of her hairstyle and her general attire. Her features and mannerisms were not particularly feminine. Although obviously quite tense, she was alert, oriented, and cooperative. After the initial tension diminished, she offered some information spontaneously. Complaints about the stepmother were rife. She was teary eyed and weepy when discussing her problems at home, and made frequent references to her desire to move to a group residence because she could not live with her aunt and uncle, who were at odds with her father. She acknowledged having no friends and that she spent most of her free time riding her bicycle, reading books, and going to the library.

During the psychiatric interview it was evident that E.F. thought frequently about her own mother and expressed a deep wish that her mother had not died. During this discussion she was again teary eyed and it took several moments for her to compose herself. She reported difficulty in sleeping at night, because once in bed she was preoccupied with the family problems. Her problem in socializing readily came to light with the remarks that though she was unhappy and lonely, she did not know how to make friends. Discussions of sex and birth resulted in considerable discomfiture, and she could not respond to questions on these subjects. When she was asked to make three wishes, she immediately responded that she wished her mother would return to life.

The psychiatrist interpreted E.F.'s productions as logical, coherent, and goal directed and there was no evidence of any thought disorder or psychotic process. The overall affect seemed appropriate to the ideational content and her general mood was one of depression.

In summary, the psychiatrist's impression was that E.F. was a reasonably bright, intact youngster, with long-standing mild-to-moderate depression, feelings of inadequacy, psychosexual role confusion, and an early passive-aggressive, passive personality structure. It was felt that she had not yet fully worked through the loss of her mother. It was also the psychiatrist's impression that the father's remarriage in the year prior to referral and to an overtly rejecting woman further complicated the difficult tasks of adolescence for this motherless child. There had also been obvious current overrejection by her father, who, in fact, appeared to be sacrificing the girl for the sake of his current marriage. This appeared to be a major factor in her current depression.

Psychological Examination

The psychologist rated E.F. as superior in general intelligence.

On the Wechsler Scale her I.Q.'s were 116 on the verbal, 122 on the performance, and 121 on the total. Considerable underlying tension, which might have lowered her capacity for sustaining attention and concentration, was noted during the examination. There was evidence of a high level of school achievement—her range of information was superior and her reading level was at grade 10.5. The psychologist stated:

> In personality organization E.F. is a highly defended but immature adolescent who struggles to maintain a withdrawal. She tends to be evasive although her thinking is reality-determined but diffuse. Most of her energies are concentrated on maintaining a defensiveness. Underlying the surface she shows considerable tension, diffuse anxiety, and deep seated feelings of inferiority about which she is very defensive.

She was reported to cope with anxiety by emotional but shallow outbursts. The psychologist was impressed with the degree of passive ambivalence which appeared in E.F.'s test record. It was interpreted that she had a deep-seated yearning for dependency and security but that she also sustained feelings of alienation and distance from her family, factors that made her feel quite frustrated. There was obvious evidence of much resentment toward her parents, particularly her stepmother.

It was stated further by the psychologist that E.F. had sustained feelings of alienation and withdrawal, which severely deprived her. Although she had some awareness of sexuality, she tended to be quite inhibited and showed considerable frustration in this area. She also showed diffuseness in differentiation of sexual role. The psychologist made a diagnosis of "withdrawal reaction of adolescence," and agreed with the social worker that placement in a residential center was the only feasible alternative.

Validation Conclusion

The Separation Anxiety Test Method apparently had succeeded in ferreting out the patterns and the problems of this girl with regard to her separation disorder and was validated by all clinical data and background material. We had, of course, formulated the problems of this case somewhat differently from the other methods of investigation. We emphasized the symbiotic nature of her problem, the anxious attachment, and the ambivalence she had been exposed to by the necessity of creating a defensive withdrawal and fantasy tactic. We strongly emphasized the conflict that had been created by the separation defensiveness, which had moved her into a loner status and into the feelings of loneliness created by the unresolved internalized attachment need. The material suggested that E.F. had continued to live in a state of internalized mourning. The death of her mother was a highly traumatic event in her life and the stepmother was unable to provide an adequate surrogate figure to aid her stepdaughter through her mourning.

The clinical emphasis in the diagnosis of this case was on passive aggressive phenomena, whereas our diagnostic impression had relied largely on the intensity of the unresolved attachment need. It seemed to us that the emphasis on the origin and the dynamic nature of this origin was of much more importance than the utilization of such concepts as passive-aggressive. Nevertheless, it is true that the intent of the diagnosis and of the case evaluation was closely similar to the material of the Separation Anxiety Test.

There was some difference of opinion with regard to placement. Because there seemed to be such good potential for psychotherapy in an out-patient setting, as shown by the Separation Anxiety Test patterns, it was thought that efforts should be made to convince the parents of the desirability of such treatment. However, unfortunately, placement needed to be effectuated because of the parents' attitude. Further, the test suggested that a small group residence might be more valuable than an institutional setting. Again the former was not feasible, and the girl was recommended for and placed in the latter setting. However, the staff agreed that she was a good candidate for therapy and she should be provided with this care in that setting. It was quite clear from the test that E.F. needed and could use a good surrogate figure to whom she could become attached.

As a footnote to this case, follow-up of this girl after a period of placement indicated complete corroboration of the test data. The social worker at the institution to which the girl was assigned could not understand why the clinic had placed her there and felt that she should have remained in a family setting, with treatment. Even in the institution she profited considerably from psychotherapy and within a short time was placed in a foster home.

CASE 3   Z.P., male aged 15½

> *An attachment-oriented adolescent with good*
> *capacity for use of personal resources but with*
> *considerable separation hostility, separation defen-*
> *siveness, and an underlying feeling of being un-*
> *loved. A case of hostile-anxious attachment with*
> *strong guilt feelings and a likely candidate for*
> *acting-out or delinquent behavior.*

Introduction

Although this case is one of an attachment-oriented individual, it depicts an adolescent boy who is not especially symbiotic, but who has a strong core to his personality. It is the type of case in which feelings of rejection and intrapunitiveness, separation defensiveness, and separation hostility play important roles. While elements of self-destructiveness are present—and they are, of course, found in individuals with depressive trends—there is considerable disturbance of the hostility system in this case. Fantasied feelings are carried out in an angry, acting-out fashion. The evidence suggested that we were dealing with fantasied resentments based upon self-rejection. In view of the strong core to the personality, the potential for dealing with these problems appeared to be good in spite of the acting-out phenomenon.

Separation Anxiety Test Results

Z.P. was examined by Dr. Alan Blumstein at Kings County Hospital in the Court Referral Project as part of a research program. Z.P. gave a total of 74 responses, which was somewhat above average. There was a good balance between the adaptive and loneliness responses, and these represented the largest area of responsiveness. Withdrawal, fantasy, and anger were the secondary areas. Without further analysis, this behavior suggested definite tendencies in the direction of sullen, withdrawn behavior as responses to separating experiences. Below this level, there was evidence of strong feelings of rejection and intrapunitiveness, since the young man gave 5 responses in each of these areas. Similarly, he showed 5 fear responses. What was also significant was an excessive difference (27 percent) between the responses to the mild and to the strong pictures, thus indicating a heightened sensitivity to intensification of separation.

An examination of the patterns of response indicated a strong attachment need of 23 percent and nearly as strong an individuation (self-reliance) of 20 percent. As noted above, this is a strong core reaction and indicates basic personality strength for development. Significant areas to be concerned with in this case were those of hostility, separation defensiveness, and the self-evaluative system, all of which showed definite evidence of disturbance. Hostility became very strong on the strong pictures, and yet there was no increase in the pain reactions. This suggested an increasing circumvention of pain response with strong stimulation, an indication that strong separations made pain too intolerable, and the shift to hostility was intense. It was also of interest that the hostility response, although containing some projection, was largely divided between anger and intrapunitiveness. This pattern strongly suggested that Z.P. would act out and at the same time be self-destructive. This combination would certainly lead to behavior unconsciously designed to seek punishment.

In line with the above, the disturbed self-evaluative pattern was significant. Here the boy showed a very high self-love loss—higher than self-esteem preoccupation—and a weak identity stress reaction. This pattern was consonant with the depressive as well as the anxious attachment categories. However, because hostility was above the norms, it fell into the hostile-anxious attachment group. He showed four out of the six characteristics seen in self-destructive adolescents (Hansburg, 1976). These included the 30 percent

Z.P. CHART FOR CONTROLLED ASSOCIATION RESPONSES

Picture Number	I	II	III	IV	V	VI	VII	VIII	IX	X	XI	XII	Total	Mild	Strong
Mental Set Response						ANSWERS NOT AVAILABLE									
Separation Intensity	S	M	M	M	M	S	M	S	M	S	S	S			
Rejection	(2)	8	15	4*	13	(10)*	14*	(11)	15	11*	(6)	(5)	5	0	5
Impaired Concentration	17	11	11	1	6	4	(11)	15	16	17	16	(15)	2	1	1
Phobic Feeling	8	(2)	(9)	3	3	3	4	(6)	(2)	15	(8)	11	5	3	2
Anxiety	9*	16	(1)	2	11	5	13	(12)	12*	(9)	2	10	3	1	2
Loneliness	(5)	(15)	(5)	16	17	(9)	6	(16)	(17)	(16)	(15)	(17)	9	3	6
Withdrawal	(3)	(12)	8	(13)	7	12	8	7	(3)	4	(9)	(14)	6	3	3
Somatic	4	14	2	10	12	11	15	8	14	7	13	7	0	0	0
Adaptive Reaction	7	(7)	(13)	(14)	(14)	(15)	(12)	(4)	(10)	(8)	(11)	(8)	11	6	5
Anger	(11)	13	14	(6)	2	(1)	5	(14)	1	1	(5)	(2)	6	1	5
Projection	10	17	3*	(17)*	8	6	9*	(1)	6	14	10	(6)	3	1	2
Empathy	16	3*	12	9*	1*	(13)	1	5	13*	(10)	(14)	12*	3	0	3
Evasion	6	1	6	5*	10	14	16	(9)	4	5	7	(4)	2	0	2
Fantasy	(14)	(10)	(7)	15*	5*	17	3	(2)	9	6	(12)	(9)	6	2	4
Well-Being	1	9	4	(8)	(16)	2	17	10*	7	3	4	1	2	2	0
Sublimation	15*	5	(16)	(7)	9	7	10	13	11	12	17*	13	2	2	0
Intrapunitive	(13)	(4)	17	12*	15	(16)*	2*	3*	(8)	13	3*	(3)	5	2	3
Identity Stress	(12)	6	10	11	4	8	7	(17)	5*	2	(1)	(16)	4	0	4
TOTAL	7	6	6	6	2	6	2	10	5	4	9	11	74	27	47

PATTERN SUMMARY CHART

RESPONSE PATTERN	Number of Responses		Total	% of Total Protocol	Area of Emphasis	Comment
	Mild II, III, IV, V, VII, IX	Strong I, VI, VIII, X, XI, XII				
Attachment (Sum of rejection loneliness, and empathy)	3	14	17	23%	Loneliness	Norm
Individuation (Sum of adaptation, well-being, and sublimation)	10	5	15	20%	Adaptation	Strong
Hostility (Sum of anger, projection and intrapunitiveness)	4	10	14	19%	Anger	Very strong Emphasis normal
Painful Tension (Sum of phobic, anxiety, and somatic reactions)	4	4	8	11%	Phobic	Weak but Emphasis normal
Reality Avoidance (Sum of withdrawal, evasion, and fantasy)	5	9	14	19%	Withdrawal and Fantasy	Strong Emphasis ambivalent
Concentration Impairment and sublimation (Self-esteem preoccupation)	1:2	1:0	2:2	5%	None	Norm
Self-love Loss (Sum of rejection and intrapunitiveness)	2	8	10	14%	Rejection and Intrapunitiveness	Strong Emphasis is A-typical
Identity Stress	0	4	4	5%	–	Weak
Absurd Responses	1	2	3	–	–	Norm
Attachment-Individuation Balance	–	–	34	46%	–	Norm
Mild-Strong Scores & %	Score 27 36%	Score 47 64%	Diff. 20	Diff. 27%	–	Slightly High

or more affect responses, high defensiveness (19 percent) and a disturbance of two subsystems in the self-evaluative area.

The type of defensive pattern seen in this case is not typical for acting-out individuals—that is, a withdrawal-fantasy combination. For this reason a more neurotic disturbance must be posited. Since hostility is strong, acting out must have a strong masochistic component. This would likely result in alternation between self-punishing acting out and depressive reaction. The constant need to assuage guilt feelings is quite apparent.

The saving features in this case lie in Z.P.'s adequate reality contact (3 absurd reactions) and in his strong personality core (high attachment and high individuation percentages). In view of these features how does it happen that he would act out in a self-punishing manner and suffer depressive reactions? It seemed likely that he might have experienced some traumatic separation events subsequent to early childhood. Unfortunately, the answers to the mental set questions were not recorded so we did not have an indication of his feelings about his past experiences. We did know that he tended to circumvent pain in favor of hostility, behavior typical of persons who have been hurt by the rejection of a parental figure. This concern with potential abandonment seemed, in this case, to lead to impulsive and self-defeating aggressive behavior. Yet the inner resources both in the establishment of positive relationships and in exploratory behavior bodes well for therapeutic intervention. His capacity for fantasy would be a useful tool in such therapy. If and when Z.P. would be led to understand his feelings of rejection, his tendency to act out angrily, and his guilty, self-defeating behavior, his disturbance would be considerably reduced.

Referral Problem

Z.P. was referred to the Court Referral Project at Kings County Hospital on 3/12/74 by the Rapid Intervention Program. The patient had been known to the court on four separate occasions: the first was on 3/10/72 for assault and possession of a deadly weapon; the second and third were on 2/1/73 and 6/20/73 on burglary charges; and the fourth was on 9/14/73 for auto theft, in which there was a finding but he was placed on probation. In view of certain aspects of his history, Z.P. was given the Separation Anxiety Test to determine to what degree separation experiences had contributed to his delinquency.

Background Material

Z.P. was one of eight siblings of black ancestry who, at the time of referral, lived in the home of Mrs. B., a black woman in her mid-thirties who was a friend of Z.P.'s family. Mrs. B's children, ranging in age from 3 to 17, lived with them. Z.P. had a girl friend, 19 years old and pregnant with Z.P.'s child, who lived with Mrs. B.'s family. Z.P.'s own siblings were either married or living independently.

The onset of Z.P.'s problems appeared to have begun when the boy was about 5 years old, at which time his own mother and father separated from each other and from the children. According to Z.P.'s natural mother, she left her husband and all the children for a man with whom she was extramaritally involved. Since that time, the mother and father had not lived together and the remaining family structure had all but disintegrated. At the time of referral the mother was living in a housing project in Brooklyn with an "aunt," a sister of the mother's boy friend. The father was unemployed and living with his own mother in Brooklyn, after having recently been evicted from his own apartment. One sibling was living with the father at the grandmother's house and another was living with an older sister.

Another significant loss Z.P. had suffered was the death of a younger brother, aged 10, when Z.P. was about 12. The younger brother had died tragically by falling off a fire escape while playing tag. Subsequently, Z.P. developed asthma, from which he continued to suffer up to the time of the referral. Whether or not this condition was related to the death of the brother was not determined. There seemed to be some suggestion in the history that the father's neglect and his alcoholism contributed in some way to the death of the younger brother.

The family of Mrs. B., with whom Z.P. lived, was on public assistance and was living in very poor surroundings. The natural mother blamed Z.P.'s problems not only on the original breakup of the family but also on the father's alcoholism. There was no evidence of delinquency or criminal activity among the other siblings or among members of Mrs. B.'s family. The natural mother reported that Z.P. had been a normal child from birth and did not show any special problems until the breakup of the family.

The social worker who interviewed Z.P. was impressed by the boy's excellent intellectual capacity because he was very articulate, although he related in a somewhat guarded but relevant manner. She reported no evidence of any apparent mental disorder.

Psychiatric Interview

The psychiatrist found Z.P. to be appropriate with no thought disorder or anything of a bizarre nature. From the boy's conversation it seemed that he was still very much attached to his mother, though accepting of the fact that she was the kind of person who could not be relied upon. He expressed love for her and a strong wish that his parents would reunite. He was defensive about his father, denying the latter's alcoholism and his unsatisfactory management of his life affairs. Z.P. spoke with appropriate sadness concerning the death of his younger brother. He still found it difficult to believe that the tragedy had occurred and expressed a strong wish to have his brother return to life. At the time of the interview, Z.P. was avoiding his former friends in a gang called the Jolly Stompers and was therefore remaining out of trouble.

His major companion at the time of referral was the 19-year-old girl with whom he was having a sex life and who also played a good maternal role for him. She had become a stable influence in his life and instructed him in proper behavior toward other adults. It was the psychiatrist's opinion that this young lady was a very influential person in his life and would be a valuable aid in any program arranged for him. Nevertheless, unresolved grief over his brother's death and the very disturbed family situation remained central problems for him. At the time of the interview Z.P. was looking forward to a job and remediation and was interested in group therapy. The psychiatrist recommended that an effort should be made to involve the mother in the boy's treatment program.

Psychological Examination

In the evaluation the psychologist included the Wechsler Intelligence Scale, Tasks of Emotional Development Test, Thematic Apperception Test, Tale-Making Test, Porteus Mazes, and the Rorschach Ink Blots. According to the psychologist, Z.P. presented himself during testing as a very sullen and withdrawn individual. He had a constant frown on his face. He cooperated with the examiner by performing all the tasks demanded of him and with a very determined facial expression, as if he wanted to do what he had to do to get it over with as quickly as possible.

The psychologist had no feeling of any emotional rapport with Z.P. After several hours with the examiner, Z.P. remained as distant as at the start. Intellectually, he functioned on both verbal and nonverbal tests in the low average range (verbal I.Q., 88, performance I.Q., 87, full-scale I.Q., 87). There was no unusual variability among the subtests, no evidence of organic brain damage, no indication of severe anxiety interfering with test performance, and no evidence of psychotic thinking.

In response to questions pertaining to social judgment, Z.P. exhibited an adequate sense of right and wrong. However, his understanding of the reasons behind social conventions was somewhat oversimplified and rigid. For example, people should not commit crimes ". . . because it's wrong." A promise should be kept ". . . because it's right to keep your word," and similar responses. He seemed unable to explain the reasons behind these ideas but did accept them nevertheless.

Further test results, particularly the Porteus Maze, suggested that basically Z.P. had good impulse control. In fact, in some ways, he was an overcontrolled person, who dealt with his problems with an exaggerated pressure on himself toward premature self-sufficiency and the periodic release of this pressure through impulsively self-destructive or self-defeating behavior. Using psychoanalytic language, the psychologist inferred that Z.P. needed to permit himself to regress in a more playful and enjoyable manner, including the experience of dependency, rather than allowing pressures to build up to the point of hostile explosiveness. (Note at this point the similarity to the separation hostility percentage on the Separation Anxiety Test.)

The psychologist considered Z.P. to be a very deprived adolescent who had felt quite rejected by others, especially his parents. However, instead of fully experiencing the pain of rejection, he had defensively reacted with tremendous hostility, much of it turned against himself. He commented that it would be of great importance to him if his therapist would encourage Z.P. to explore some of his painful feelings. He felt that until he was fully able to experience and work through painful feelings of loss and rejection, he would continue to react with rage as well as intrapunitive feelings.

The test data further suggested that in addition to quite natural feelings of sadness and loneliness in response to the losses he had experienced in his life, and in addition to the anger and intrapunitiveness discussed above, Z.P. had reacted to the various rejections in his life with an abnormally high degree of withdrawal from other people. His typical modes of withdrawal included avoidance of close involvement with other people and a retreat into fantasy. This withdrawal was perhaps the most pathological aspect of Z.P.'s functioning and deserved the serious attention of his therapist.

Z.P. occasionally feared men as potentially dangerous and, perhaps, even murderous. This fear may have been related to his perception of his father's role in the death of his brother. When interacting with peers, he tended to feel rejected by them. Even when functioning in a leadership role in a group, he would feel internally alone, sad, and unacceptable.

In response to the deprivations he had undergone, Z.P. felt that he could not count on being nurtured by his mother or any other woman. He sometimes fantasied that he might receive from a wife the love and caring he did not receive from his mother, although he expected such love and caring from a woman to be incomplete, temporary, and not fully real. If any woman would act nurturantly toward him, he probably would view her as being merely charitable. Fortunately, beneath all these problems, Z.P. did have a basic capacity for forming good interprersonal relationships, which was an important strength in his personality.

Z.P. was determined to succeed in life. Much of his determination seemed to be directed toward school work. He sometimes found the pressure of academic achievement very stressful and would react by feeling uncomfortable and tired; however, he would generally counteract these feelings by pushing himself even harder toward completion of his work.

Thus, Z.P. was a person with many strengths. Despite his withdrawal from other people, underneath he had a basic capacity for forming good interpersonal relationships. His delinquent behavior was seen as reflecting, not a person who lacked self-control, but rather one who was so overcontrolled and who put so many pressures and demands on himself that he would occasionally release the pressure through impulsive or antisocial, self-defeating behavior. Furthermore, the hostility he directed against others and against himself was seen as an expression of unresolved rage over the separations he had experienced in his life (rejection by parents and the death of his brother) and as a substitute for the more healthy expression of pain over these experiences.

Ongoing Treatment and Current Status

Z.P. had been and was (at the time of this study) involved in four components of the Court Referral Project. The focus of the individual treatment modality had been generally supportive, designed to evince feelings of trust and confidence on the part of Z.P. for the worker. Moreover, as of late, the individual treatment modality had shifted focus and moved toward the point at which Z.P. was verbalizing material of a more valuable and personal nature. In addition to the above, the therapist had begun to see the father on a once-a-week therapeutic basis, while Z.P. was being seen on an intensive basis by another worker. It was planned to eventually develop a conjoint treatment program for Z.P., which would include Z.P.'s 19-year-old girl friend. In comparison to his previous lack of involvement, his poor attendance, and delinquent behavior, Z.P. had made great strides in everything in which he was involved. He had achieved a position of group leader, as previously mentioned, and was now heavily entrenched in the individual treatment modality.

He had shown marked improvement in areas of work and in the development of interpersonal relationships. Moreover, Z.P. had taken an active, participatory interest in the recreational offerings of the program. He had also shown considerable growth in school in the areas of mathematics and reading and his behavior in the classroom was seen as appropriate.

Validation Conclusion

In the case of Z.P. the Separation Anxiety Test showed a remarkable similarity to the material obtained by the clinic staff at Kings County Hospital. The corroboration was focused not only on the separations and serious loss he had experienced but also on the personality characteristics he subsequently demonstrated. There was considerable correlation between the test and the reports of the social worker, psychologist, and psychiatrist, especially in the areas of acting out, fantasy, feelings of rejection, intrapunitiveness, and depressed feelings in relation to the rejection. The extent of his hostility was quite recognizable by all. The content material of his background indicated the reason why this boy showed such patterns on the Separation Anxiety Test. Of further importance was the strength of the core of his personality structure, as was very well demonstrated by the Separation Anxiety Test. As it turned out, this factor was of great predictive value with regard to the subsequent improvement achieved by therapeutic intervention. This was an unusually striking case of clinical validation for the Separation Anxiety Test.

CASE 4 V.L., Male, aged 15

An adolescent with a poor personality core (low attachment and low individuation), demonstrating a dependent detachment-separation disorder. This is characteristic of the dependent narcissistic personality, a character structure with limited life success patterns.

Introduction

This case is an example of an adolescent boy with a poor personality core, in which there is difficulty in forming close relationships, and at the same time with inadequate use of personal resources. Such a separation pattern is frequently associated with dependent individuals who rely largely on narcissistic gratifications and who hold on to their environments because of their essential fear that they will not be able to utilize their resources in new environments. While a symbiotic phenomenon underlies this feeling, it nevertheless results in a disorder of the character structure, which makes it necessary for him to recruit individuals to gratify his dependency needs but does not contribute much to a relationship. V.L. meets the critieria for dependent detachment.

Furthermore, the case is an example of a youngster who has had inadequate separation experiences from his family, despite the fact that the family is not a particularly nourishing one. As pointed out in the preceding case, deficiencies of this type are not common on the Separation Anxiety Test. Dependent detached personalities tend to have very limited life success patterns.

As often seen in these cases, there is an enormous amount of affect as well as evasion in relation to separation experiences. This condition, combined with borderline reality testing, a symbiotic factor, and a low self-evaluative system, adds a depressive tone to the narcissistic character structure.

Separation Anxiety Test Results

V.L. came readily to the examination, seemed to have some preliminary reservations, and was confused by the instructions. It was

V.L. CHART FOR CONTROLLED ASSOCIATION RESPONSES

Picture Number	I	II	III	IV	V	VI	VII	VIII	IX	X	XI	XII	Total	Mild	Strong
Mental Set Response	N	Y	Y	Y	N	Y	Y	N	N	N	N	Y		4	1
Separation Intensity	S	M	M	M	M	S	M	S	M	S	S	S	5		
Rejection	(2)	8	15	4*	(13)	10*	14*	(11)	15	11*	(6)	(5)	5	1	4
Impaired Concentration	(17)	11	(11)	1	(6)	4	(11)	15	16	(17)	(16)	15	6	3	3
Phobic Feeling	(8)	(2)	(9)	3	(3)	3	(4)	(6)	(2)	15	(8)	11	8	5	3
Anxiety	(9)*	16	(1)	2	(11)	(5)	(13)	12	12*	9	(2)	10	6	3	3
Loneliness	5	15	5	(16)	17	9	(6)	(16)	(17)	16	(15)	(17)	6	3	3
Withdrawal	3	12	8	13	(7)	12	(8)	7	3	(4)	(9)	14	4	2	2
Somatic	4	14	2	10	12	11	15	(8)	14	7	13	7	1	0	1
Adaptive Reaction	7	7	13	14	14	(15)	(12)	4	10	8	11	8	2	1	1
Anger	11	13	14	6	(2)	1	(5)	(14)	1	(1)	5	(2)	5	2	3
Projection	10	(17)	3*	17*	8	(6)	9*	(1)	6	(14)	10	6	4	1	3
Empathy	16	3*	12	9*	1*	13	1	5	13*	10	(14)	12*	1	0	1
Evasion	6	(1)	6	(5)*	10	14	16	9	4	5	(7)	(4)	5	3	2
Fantasy	14	10	7	15*	5*	17	3	(2)	9	6	12	9	1	0	1
Well-Being	1	9	4	8	16	2	17	10*	7	3	4	1	0	0	0
Sublimation	15*	(5)	(16)	(7)	9	7	10	13	11	12	17*	13	3	3	0
Intrapunitive	13	4	17	12*	15	(6)*	2*	3*	(8)	13	(3)*	3	3	1	2
Identity Stress	(12)	6	(10)	11	4	(8)	(7)	17	5*	(2)	(1)	(16)	7	2	5
TOTAL	5	4	6	3	6	5	8	7	3	5	10	5	67	30	37

104

V.L.
PATTERN SUMMARY CHART

RESPONSE PATTERN	Number of Responses		Total	% of Total Protocol	Area of Emphasis	Comment
	Mild II, III, IV, V, VII, IX	Strong I, VI, VIII, X, XI, XII				
Attachment (Sum of rejection, loneliness, and empathy)	4	8	12	18%	Loneliness	Weak but typical emphasis
Individuation (Sum of adaptation, well-being, and sublimation)	4	1	5	7%	Sublimation	Very weak and abnormal emphasis
Hostility (Sum of anger, projection and intrapunitiveness)	4	8	12	18%	Anger	Strong but Emphasis normal
Painful Tension (Sum of phobic, anxiety, and somatic reactions)	8	7	15	22%	Phobic	Very strong, Emphasis typical
Reality Avoidance (Sum of withdrawal, evasion, and fantasy)	5	5	10	15%	Withdrawal and Fantasy	Strong, Emphasis abnormal
Concentration Impairment and sublimation (Self-esteem preoccupation)	3:3	3:0	6:3	13%	Concentration Impairment	Strong, Intellectual problems
Self-love Loss (Sum of rejection and intrapunitiveness)	2	6	8	12%	Rejection Intrapunitiveness	Excessive Emphasis is A-typical
Identity Stress	2	5	7	10%	–	Norm
Absurd Responses	1	3	4	–	–	Borderline
Attachment-Individuation Balance	–	–	21	31%	–	Mild picture problem
Mild-Strong Scores & %	Score 30 45%	Score 37 55%	Diff. 7	Diff. 10%	–	Weak: poor judgment

necessary to review the instructions twice in order to clarify for him the nature of the task involved. Throughout the examination, he seemed more blasé and defensive than overtly anxious. He was responsive and reacted readily to each picture.

V.L. produced a total of 67 responses, which is on the higher end of the average range and is considered to be a cooperative effort. There were 30 responses on the mild pictures and 37 on the strong pictures, with a difference of only 10 percent between the two. This figure is much below the usual 20 percent average and suggested poor judgment and discrimination. He reacted especially strongly to the picture of the death of the mother and, secondarily, to the brother leaving on a voyage. His strong reaction to the judge picture was within normal limits. The very strong reaction to the death of the mother was considered to be a symbiotic indicator and was followed by other such indicators. There were only 5 out of 12 "yes" answers to the mental set questions. Since this number was less than average, it suggested a child who had not had many separation experiences from his home. It is also noteworthy that he showed a relatively large number of reactions to the new neighborhood picture as well as to the camp picture. Thus, many of the mild pictures produced a large number of reactions, especially those of fear and anxiety.

There were 4 projection responses, which was definitely not typical for the hostility area. This, combined with the number of intrapunitive responses, indicated a strong need to blame someone, either others or himself, for separating experiences. Another noteworthy characteristic was the relative infrequency of adaptive responses (2). This is atypical and indicated a severe resistance to adapting to any separating experience.

The examination of the patterns was quite revealing with regard to this boy's personality and his problems of separation. The most significant fact was the impoverishment of the personality, as demonstrated by the below-average attachment percentage and the extremely low level of the individuation percentage. Inadequate relatedness and poor use of personal resources were suggested by this indicator, and was a negative factor for therapeutic intervention. It was also noteworthy that V.L. offered the equivalent number of attachment as individuation responses to the mild pictures. This is a known symbiotic factor and is often found in depressive as well as self-destructive behavior.

One of the most startling aspects of this record was the very strong affect reaction, 40 percent separation hostility and pain (22 percent separation pain and 18 percent hostility). Since these reactions appeared in a relatively impoverished personality, this boy would depend largely on his own poor resources. Therefore, he would flail helplessly with feelings of inability to cope with situations presented to him. Such a large percentage of affect reactions is found in individuals who, in the face of separation, tend to feel self-destructive. It also suggests that V.L. would act out, since the basic core is not strong enough to prevent this behavior.

A somewhat high percentage in the defensive system was shown (15 percent) and was dominated by evasion. This unrealistic approach to the problems of separation was heightened by the four inappropriate or absurd responses, where only two or three are average. Such a condition is also found in youngsters with depressive reactions as well as self-destructive tendencies.

In the self-evaluative system, self-love loss was considerable (12 percent), which included a total of 5 feelings of rejection and 3 intrapunitive responses. Such a sense of unworthiness suggested that V.L. had incorporated into his personality a sense of hopelessness about himself. Weaknesses in the concentration area were also indicated, thus suggesting that he would have problems in coping with intellectual tasks under separation and that he would have difficulty in school. The necessity to act out his problems as indicated by comparison between the object-relatedness and the individuation core of his personality, coupled with impairment of concentration, indicated that he would either avoid school or do very poorly if he did attend. He would be greatly discouraged by intellectual operations.

Although identity stress was within normal limits, it was still at the bottom of the norm. This result, combined with the aspects of the self-evaluative system noted above, further corroborated the weakness in this area.

In summary, the patterns of the Separation Anxiety Test indicated a combination of poor personality core, with weak levels in the use of resources and adaptations to relationships. There was an underlying depressive tone and strong affect levels, borderline reality testing, evasiveness, and intellectual problems—all indicating inappropriate acting out. An underlying symbiotic problem, a need to blame himself and others, and considerable difficulty in facing separation situations were evident. Thus, diagnostically he fell into the category of dependent detachment characterized by immaturity and inadequacy, probably egosyntonic in nature. Technically, the test suggested a traditional diagnosis of immature character structure with depressive and hostile factors.

It appeared that the treatment of choice would be placement away from his present setting, even though there was considerable separation affect. It was obvious that the present home setting could not possibly be encouraging of positive personality traits because it was inducing intense feelings of rejection and inadequacy. The indications were that attempts at psychotherapy would be difficult and long term, and that milieu treatment would have better, though still limited, success. The test results suggested that considerable persuasion would be required to get V.L. to accept placement, since he had such a strong emotional affect in relation to separation, although much of this was on a narcissistic basis. Therefore, the author's preference in this case was for residential treatment.

Referral Problem

V.L. was referred to the Jewish Child Care Association by his mother at the suggestion of a friend whose own daughter had been placed at he Hawthorne Cedar Knolls School. The mother's chief complaints at the time of the initial inquiry were truancy, poor school performance, and bad companions. According to the mother, school problems dated back to the fourth grade. V.L. had attended a mental health clinic in the previous year but only for a few sessions. During the referral period the author administered the Separation Anxiety Test to the boy.

Background Material

V.L. was an only child whose mother was 40 and whose father was 50. The parents had been married 19 years. The father was unemployed and the family subsisted on disability insurance. The family had been seen by the Jewish Child Care Association* on a previous occasion but had then broken several subsequent appointments. However, later on, it appeared that the mother had brought the boy to the Brooklyn Family Court and had been referred to the Jewish Board of Guardians. The latter agency, in turn, referred the youngster to JCCA for placement. Because the mother could not force the boy to accept placement, she had taken out a PINS (person in need of supervision) petition. The court worker did not feel that a PINS petition was necessary or warranted and advised voluntary placement with JCCA. One of the problems of referral had been the father's refusal to come for a second interview.

As seen by the JCCA caseworker, V.L. was a short, chubby, cute blond boy, who seemed younger than his stated age both in appearance and in manner. He showed strong signs of anxiety and depression and manifested a poor sense of self. His defenses seemed primitive and easily penetrated and the caseworker observed that he was an isolated, lonely boy overwhelmed by frustration and a sense of futility about his family situation. He was easily brought to tears when he talked about his family. He minimized his school problems, but seemed to be in touch with his rage at his parents' inadequacy.

He showed extremely rigid feelings toward his parents. For example, he said, "My father doesn't make it as a father; he always makes a fool of himself." These criticisms were understandable, because the father was a compulsive gambler. The boy cited times when the father would take money from him and stated that his father often kept very late hours. He alluded to an embezzling incident involving some merchandise from Israel and how his father was apprehended because he was so stupid. "If I stole a thousand dollars, my father would probably do nothing, but if I don't go with him some place, he'd beat me up."

His feelings toward his mother were much more diffuse, somewhat hostile and protective at the same time. He voiced little positive regard toward anyone. His awareness of his own behavior in the light of the family problems was that it kept his father in line.

From this point on JCCA will be used occasionally to represent Jewish Child Care Association.

The boy had memories of violent arguments between his parents and threats of divorce. Although he admitted to being unhappy at home, he did not want placement. He worried that his father might leave his mother, and expressed concern that his·mother would be left alone. The latter feeling was seen as a probable rationalization for his own wish to remain at home.

When seen as a unit, each member of the family kept a strong hold on his/her feelings with occasional outbursts. The boy found it most difficult to keep quiet. In response to any complaint from his father about him, he would counter with outrage and tears. The family seemed to have no visible alliances. The mother and father were not united and the boy was detached from each. In fact, according to the social worker, he seemed to be depersonalized by his parents and they perceived him as a perpetual infant. Although he expressed various feelings, neither mother nor father was able to respond to his unfolding personality. When the boy brought up the father's gambling, the mother started to cry. This infuriated the father, who countered that his wife was a neurotic who didn't let the boy touch her and had not given the boy any affection. It was difficult to gain insight into what was transpiring, since both parents seemed to talk around issues and only hinted at problems. It was a strong investment for both to keep quiet or else there was a counterattack on some highly charged issue.

When V.L. was being interviewed, the mother walked up and down the hall, seemingly in an effort to catch some of the conversation. The boy was less unobtrusive and his shadow could be seen against the glass. It was very difficult to get an adequate history, because both parents were so withholding. In a phone conversation, the mother had expressed concern with V.L.'s inappropriate behavior (he would often jump on her as though he was a baby). In the background, while the conversation was proceeding, the father could be heard saying that she shouldn't be telling the worker things like that.

There was a strong sexual component to V.L.'s behavior described above by his mother, but she would not elaborate on it. The mother seemed to be a very depressed woman with little awareness of her own conflicts, nor did she show any motivation for change. There was an egosyntonic quality about her personality and she generally showed hostility at being interviewed. The father was there only because his wife asked him to be. The caseworker's impression of V.L. was that of an infantile, depressed boy who was having difficulties in all areas of his life. He impressed her as a somewhat dull child, and it was difficult for her to assess how much his emotional problems had affected his learning capacity. Because of the strained home environment, Geller house (center for adolescents) was considered an interim placement, where a diagnostic work-up could be completed. However, V.L.'s immaturity and resistance to placement made this questionable. The caseworker had the feeling that placement at Pleasantville would be more appropriate than one geared for an older adolescent.

Psychiatric Interview

The psychiatrist had referred V.L. for a Separation Anxiety Test. He was concerned about the degree of separation anxiety in the boy and his fear of leaving the home environment. The psychiatrist found V.L. to be somewhat infantile in his manner of talking, fidgety, distractible, and lacking in spontaneity. There was evidence that the boy was concerned about his impulse control, as was manifested by his reaction to a disturbance which had occurred in his classroom. It was very difficult for the boy to indicate any of his own contributions to his problems, either at home or at school.

The psychiatrist found V.L. to be very concerned about his mother's nervous, difficult behavior and his father's gambling. He had developed a defense against his father's model as a gambler, by holding on to a certain amount of money in his pocket. The psychiatrist sensed, however, that the boy displayed a curiosity and excitement toward gambling. V.L. felt that although he had been identified as the patient in the family, he suggested that the whole family was disturbed. The boy verbalized how impressed he had been by the violent arguments between his parents over the years. He expressed the feeling that his parents' marriage would not last if he were removed from his home.

Moreover, it was noted that the boy presented egocentric, magical, and even omnipotent thinking and that he was quite burdened with these feelings. What emerged was the sense of responsibility for maintaining at least superficially an intact family and attempting in his own mind to reconstruct a more efficient and cohesive family unit.

The psychiatrist was also impressed with the fact that each time V.L. had gone to camp, one of his grandparents had died. To quote from the report: "The issue of separation anxiety clearly emerged; V.L. gave hints of fearing that, for example, an accident might befall his father or his mother if he were not around and available to check up." To illustrate the extent of his omnipotent and magical thinking, V.L. related that he was a jinx and that he was the only one who "came out," in reference to his mother's previous miscarriages. The boy spoke at length about unresolved dependency needs and about his loneliness. He had no one to confide in, such as an older brother (see his reaction to the picture of the older brother going on a voyage in the Separation Anxiety Test), or someone with whom to share secrets; he made statements indicating that he felt a sense of competition and left out in relation to his parents. It was interesting that V.L. expressed a desire to have a brother, even an adopted one. He also added that he wanted a job and once having developed a sufficient bank account, he would not have to depend upon his parents for money.

The psychiatrist was unable to elicit any evidence of a thinking or a psychotic disorder. The major mood indicated was one of tension and anxiety, but additional depressive elements were also indicated. What impressed the psychiatrist was the fact that while on the surface insights and judgments appeared limited, it seemed that ultimately, if V.L. became more relaxed and secure, he would become more highly verbal and would present more significant and workable material.

In an interview with the parents, the psychiatrist was impressed with their depression and their desire to have the boy out of the home. They were bothered by his bossiness and at the same time by his immaturity. He related mainly to younger children instead of to those of his own age. The mother often referred to the masochistic, self-destructive characteristics displayed by V.L., mentioning that he recently cut himself with a razor and had taken some of his mother's Valium, obviously resulting in an overreaction. The parents took him to the emergency room of a hospital, assuming that he was a heavy, hard-drug user. The evidence seemed to indicate, however, that V.L. was attempting a pseudoadult role, which was beyond him.

The psychiatrist's diagnostic reaction to V.L. was that he showed a behavior disorder of adolescence with passive-aggressive but also neurotic elements of a phobic-anxious and depressive nature. The psychiatrist stated: "Clearly there will be a process necessary to aid V.L. in working through the separation anxiety he experiences in order to allow him to accept residential treatment center placement, which seems indicated. There is obviously a need for corrective therapy in a milieu program, highly structured, supportive, and definitive to make inroads into resolution of conflict between dependency and separation-individuation to allow this youngster to move into a more typical phase of middle adolescence, which he has failed to do thus far."

Psychological Examination

Although V.L. obtained I.Q.'s of 94 and 92, it was estimated that his true intelligence was in the bright normal range. He showed much instability in functioning, missing easy items and attaining good scores on more difficult ones. Generally, he showed very immature and impulsive judgment. In practical situations, he was still egocentrically oriented, like a young child. He frequently demonstrated poor frustration tolerance, which lowered his proficiency. Educationally he functioned poorly, having reading and arithmetic levels of 6.3 and 5.6, respectively.

The psychologist was impressed with V.L.'s impulsive personality organization and immaturity, and he projected many adolescent developmental tensions. To quote: "He is a highly egocentrically oriented child. His thinking is diffuse but usually reality determined. He shows conformity but, because of his egocentricity, he tends to be indulgent and subjectively oriented. There is a considerable amount of agitation and depression." It was the psychologist's opinion that the boy was experiencing intense, unresolved passive-aggressive tensions, which were reinforced in this developmental period. On the one hand, he strove to be assertive, which was a positive facet; on the other hand, he was strongly involved with his parents, particularly his mother, involvement that aroused much agitation and frustration. In a social role, he verbalized appropriate identity values.

Further discussion by the psychologist emphasized a pervasive instability. He was highly cynical, which is associated with sophistication, and yet he was also immature. His stories on the TAT were largely about rebellious children. There was evidence that he fought with his parents, more particularly his mother, and that he was ambivalent toward his father. It appeared that his involvement with his mother was handicapping his sexual identity. His anger toward his mother protected an underlying, diffuse identification with her. He displayed a deep yearning for passivity, against which he defended himself by a reinforcement of assertiveness and defiance, which usually ended in a masochistic solution.

The psychologist made a diagnosis of behavior disorder of adolescence and said that V.L. would benefit from a residential treatment such as Hawthorne-Cedar Knolls. There seemed to be some difference of opinion between the psychologist on the one hand and the psychiatrist and the social worker on the other with regard to the kind of placement for this boy. The social worker and the psychiatrist both felt that V.L. needed a treatment center in which there were predominantly younger children and adolescents with less sophistication. The difference of opinion appeared in part to be related to the boy's immature personality, the need for improvement in his self-identity, as well as his depressive and masochistic tendencies.

Validation Conclusion

In this case, the Separation Anxiety Test appeared to emphasize certain elements that were not so strongly emphasized in the other examinations. The inadequate personality characteristics of this boy, which included the poor use both of relationships and of his personal resources, suggested a more egosyntonic characteristic of V.L.'s personality than was indicated by the other examinations. The Separation Anxiety Test did not see this as a developmental crisis but rather as a more fundamental one. However, there was general agreement that an enormous amount of separation affect existed. The intensity of the separation pain and of the separation hostility was so great as to be considered pathological.

It was evident that V.L. was being forced, and had been forced for a long time, to depend largely on narcissistic elements. This pervaded the Separation Anxiety Test Record. Although this evidence appeared to some extent in the other interviews and examinations, it was not emphasized to the degree noted in the Separation Anxiety Test. The strong masochistic and depressive elements in his personality showed up rather strongly in the latter test and confirmed the opinions of the other workers.

From the Separation Anxiety Test, it seemed unlikely that this boy would profit from insight forms of therapy. This was indicated by the very low scores in the areas of attachment and individuation (self-reliance), a known contraindication for therapy. Yet the clinic workers were all in agreement with regard to therapeutic intervention, although within a residential treatment setting. No material is available on the eventual outcome of this case.

The test indicated that V.L.'s relationship to adults would be largely dependent and unstable and that V.L. would need both structure from and dependency upon benign adult figures. His own dependency needs would probably continually influence his behavior. There was no doubt that V.L. was searching for models, especially a slightly older male figure (which was suggested by his reaction to the picture of the older brother leaving on a voyage). There was general agreement that placement in a residential treatment center was essential in order that V.L. escape the rejection, neglect, and dissension in his own family.

CASE 5 L.S., Female, aged 16½

> *An adolescent girl with a history of traumatic separations, whose personality has obviously been seriously damaged and whose character structure is narcissistic and dependent and, similar to Case 4, has limited capacity for close personal ties and for the use of personal resources. This is another case of dependent detachment.*

Introduction

This case is an example of a girl who has difficulties in forming close relationships but who nevertheless has strong needs that remain ungratified and who obviously has developed a narcissistic character structure. The case is of further interest because of the girl's limited use of personal resources in the individuation area. Thus, it is another good illustration of a very poor separation-individuation core. In this case the reliance on narcissism alone apparently leaves the girl exposed to a considerable amount of phobic reactions.

Additionally, this girl further illustrates how some individuals deal with traumatic separations occurring early in life. As previously stated this type of pattern is far less common than those in which there is a high attachment in comparison to individuation (self-reliance) or a high individuation level in comparison to attachment. As in Case 4 personalities of this type move in a direction of very limited life performance both in their human relations and in their constructive use of resources.

Further, such individuals may develop defenses of guardedness and evasion in order to avoid any depth in their relationships. To achieve narcissistic gratification, such persons would necessarily have surface relationships with strong protective persons, but because of the absence of depth of the relationships, it would be obvious that any person offering narcissistic gratifications would be easily accepted into a relationship in preference to any others. Therefore, it would be expected that individuals of this type would accept relationships with anyone who offered such gratifications without making too many demands on the relationship.

Separation Anxiety Test Results

L.S. came to the examination readily, seemed interested in the procedure but did not verbalize. She simply responded to any questions asked of her. She was an attractive girl, thoroughly rouged and powdered, and smiling sheepishly. During the examination she demonstrated no overt anxiety, but, in general, gave the impression of being a girl who kept her own counsel.

L.S. gave a total of 44 responses, which is less than average and indicates some degree of guardedness and constriction. It was noteworthy that she responded with 10 "yeses" to the mental set questions, an indication of intrapsychic and geographic separations of considerable intensity and frequency. She gave 21 responses to the mild pictures and 23 to the strong pictures, an indication of poor judgment and discrimination quite similar to that of Case 4. This is a frequent finding in individuals with pathological character structures. The number of responses to each picture showed little variation in frequency, and she gave no responses at all to areas of rejection, impaired concentration, sublimation, intrapunitiveness, and identity stress. These reactions were further evidence of guardedness and constriction. The most intense areas were those of fear and evasion, indicating a phobic orientation with a strong denial of need. This condition is further suggested by only 5 loneliness responses and just as many anger responses. The evidence from a study of the various single categories suggested a rather limited personality structure with a greater tendency toward affect, a denial of closeness, and an evasion of her true feelings.

A study of the patterns revealed that the attachment level was poor (16 percent), thus indicating a fear of closeness and avoidance of close relationships. At the same time the individuation level was very low (11 percent). As in Case 4 this pattern reflected a serious impoverishment of the personality, a low capacity for in-depth relationships, and poor use of personal resources. A further significant pathological factor was in the defensive system, in which strong denial and evasion were prominent features. The

L.S. CHART FOR CONTROLLED ASSOCIATION RESPONSES

Picture Number	I	II	III	IV	V	VI	VII	VIII	IX	X	XI	XII	Total	Mild	Strong
Mental Set Response	Y	Y	Y	Y	Y	Y	N	Y	Y	Y	N	Y			
Separation Intensity	S	M	M	M	M	S	M	S	M	S	S	S	10	5	5
Rejection	2	8	15	4*	13	10*	14*	11	15	11*	6	5	0	0	0
Impaired Concentration	17	11	11	1	6	4	11	15	16	17	16	15	0	0	0
Phobic Feeling	8	(2)	9	(3)	3	(3)	(4)	(6)	(2)	15	(8)	(11)	8	4	4
Anxiety	9*	16	(1)	2	11	5	13	(12)	12*	(9)	(2)	10	4	1	3
Loneliness	(5)	15	(5)	16	17	9	6	16	(17)	(16)	15	(17)	5	2	3
Withdrawal	3	12	8	(13)	7	12	8	7	(3)	4	9	14	2	2	0
Somatic	(4)	14	(2)	10	12	11	(15)	8	14	7	(13)	7	4	2	2
Adaptive Reaction	(7)	(7)	(13)	14	14	15	(12)	4	10	8	11	8	4	3	1
Anger	11	(13)	14	(6)	2	(1)	5	(14)	1	1	5	(2)	5	2	3
Projection	10	17	3*	17*	8	6	9*	1	6	(14)	10	6	1	0	1
Empathy	16	3*	12	9*	1*	(13)	1	5	13*	(10)	14	12*	2	0	2
Evasion	6	(1)	(6)	(5*)	10	14	16	(9)	(4)	5	(7)	(4)	7	4	3
Fantasy	14	10	7	15*	5*	17	3	(2)	9	6	12	9	1	0	1
Well-Being	1	9	4	8	(16)	2	17	10*	7	3	4	1	1	1	0
Sublimation	15*	5	16	7	9	7	10	13	11	12	17*	13	0	0	0
Intrapunitive	13	4	17	12*	15	16*	2*	3*	8	13	3*	3	0	0	0
Identity Stress	12	6	10	11	4	8	7	17	5*	2	1	16	0	0	0
TOTAL	3	4	5	4	1	3	3	5	4	4	4	4	44	21	23

118

PATTERN SUMMARY CHART

RESPONSE PATTERN	Number of Responses		Total	% of Total Protocol	Area of Emphasis	Comment
	Mild II, III, IV, V, VII, IX	Strong I, VI, VIII, X, XI, XII				
Attachment (Sum of rejection, loneliness, and empathy)	2	5	7	16%	Loneliness	Weak but Emphasis typical
Individuation (Sum of adaptation, well-being, and sublimation)	4	1	5	11%	Adaptation	Weak but Emphasis typical
Hostility (Sum of anger, projection and intrapunitiveness)	2	4	6	14%	Anger	Norm
Painful Tension (Sum of phobic, anxiety, and somatic reactions)	7	9	16	36%	Phobic	Unusually excessive Emphasis O.K.
Reality Avoidance (Sum of withdrawal, evasion, and fantasy)	6	4	10	23%	Evasion and Fantasy	Unusually excessive, Emphasis abnormal
Concentration Impairment and sublimation (Self-esteem preoccupation)	0:0	0:0	0	0%	None	Unusually low
Self-love Loss (Sum of rejection and intrapunitiveness)	0	0	0	0%	None Intrapunitiveness	Unusually low
Identity Stress	0	0	0	0%	–	Unusually low
Absurd Responses	1	0	1	–	–	Norm
Attachment-Individuation Balance	–	–	14	32%	–	Fair
Mild-Strong Scores & %	Score 21 47%	Score 23 52%	Diff. 2	Diff. 5%	–	Very low

119

highest level of reaction was in the fear-anxiety-pain system, in which she produced 36 percent of her responses. Thus, despite feeling this intensity of affect, her disturbed defensive system and her narcissistic functioning not only limit her capacity for closeness but also leave her exposed to specific fears—she selected the phobic response on 8 out of the 12 pictures.

Her complete denial of any effect of separation upon her self-evaluative system was further evidence of a strong narcissistic orientation. This is a pathological pattern and, in addition to the above, suggests that L.S. will not deal directly with the developmental requirements of adolescence and will thus miss the rich opportunities for growth in a number of significant areas. Any relationship would be handled superficially.

Nearly 75 percent of her responses were either in the affect area or in the defensive system. When this is combined with the poor personality core, we expect considerable impulsive acting out. She would not permit sufficient closeness to deal with these internalized disturbances. On the basis of our diagnostic formulations (Chapter I), we can characterize this case as one of dependent detachment. Using typical psychiatric terminology, a diagnostic appraisal suggests a narcissistic, immature character disorder with a poorly developed separation-individuation process. It is likely that at times she might become depressed if she is unable to gratify her narcissistic needs. At such times she may also be somewhat self-destructive, since four out of the six such factors are present in the record. Ultimately, it seems probable that L.S. would indulge in some form of self-harm, possibly drugs, although her phobic reactions suggest that she may be frightened of such acting out.

Because of her difficulty in using her resources as well as her attachments, she is likely to avoid the help that she obviously needs. Therefore, the author did not recommend therapeutic assistance but rather a structured environment and milieu treatment. It seemed doubtful that this girl knew where her best interests lay.

Referral Problem

At the time the author saw L.S. for the Separation Anxiety Test, she had been in placement with the Jewish Child Care Association for 11 years. Her original placement when she was nearly 6 years old was in a foster home. When she was 11, she was replaced into a group residence because the foster mother complained of the girl's difficulties in relating to a family situation. Some time later L.S. was transferred from the group residence to an older group residence. During the course of her placement, she had had some therapy for a year and had then withdrawn. Flight from places, situations, and people had been a constant characteristic of L.S.'s behavior during her placement with the agency. The purpose of providing a Separation Anxiety Test at the time of referral was to illustrate the use of the method in helping the social worker deal with the problem of interviewing this girl in the residence. The direction these interviews would take was an important part of the referral.

Background Material

Although the author offered some history in the referral problem, the purpose of the history was to explain the referral. This background is now presented in greater detail.

L.S. was the youngest of three children, all of whom had been referred to the agency for placement. At the time of referral L.S. was nearly 5 years old and placement had been initiated through the Family Court. The father had died two years before referral, and several months after the father's death, the mother became involved with another man. Because the mother neglected her children, a maternal uncle brought the situation to the attention of the court. The court remanded the mother to a mental hospital for a diagnostic work-up and paroled the children to the uncle, who then applied for placement. The diagnostic work-up on the mother indicated that she was suffering from organic brain damage, had poor social judgment, and little insight. She was not considered psychotic. The children lived a short time with their relatives before the court placed them. Prior to the death of the father, the family had been intact, although the father, a mail handler, was considered to be schizophrenic.

During the period from ages 5 through 9, L.S. experienced a number of significant changes in her life. These included two foster home placements, two group residences, twelve different social workers, and two therapists. When L.S. was about 10 years old, her mother died. Thus, it could be stated that by the time she had reached the age of 14, she had been traumatized by an unusual number of separating experiences, including the death of her mother. During all this time she demonstrated a strong need for attention as well as visible indications of needing to be wanted. Yet she was unable to adequately utilize the attentions and interest that were showered upon her because of her obviously attractive appearance but needful manner.

From early beginnings in her placements and in her therapeutic experiences L.S. impressed adults as being warm and related, but these characteristics always turned out to be superficial ones. Frequently, when a person made an effort to reciprocate L.S.'s seeming friendliness, the girl fled from the relationship. This behavior was particularly true where men were concerned but it was also evident in her relationships with women. At different stages during this period of her life she moved from depressed states or moods into excited volubility and then would readily withdraw from contact. Earlier, in family situations, she made superficial adjustments considered to be good by both teachers and foster parents, but these impressions later yielded to others not so favorable. Another characteristic noted by all who saw her, including psychiatrists, was her phobic reactions in her behavior as well as in her dreams.

During all this time L.S. had been especially close to a sister who was 10 years older. The sister often visited L.S. in the foster home and L.S. would, in turn, visit her sister in the latter's apartment. While the mother was alive, contacts with her own family were sporadic; there had been a special problem centering around the mother's paramour, for whom L.S. apparently had a considerable terror. The history had shown that L.S. had sometimes been exposed to sexual behavior between her mother and her paramour, and had occasionally even slept in the same bed with them. The social worker reported that L.S. had developed a fear of men "for no apparent reason," although the history strongly emphasized the basis for the morbid fear.

This fear had been displaced to one of her foster fathers, who for five years had tried to have a close relationship with her but to no avail. When she was 9½, the foster parents reported that L.S. was not only moody and sulky but also always appeared angry about something. The social worker stated that "she seemed to want everybody's individual attention, was extremely sensitive, and easily felt rejected." L.S. had great difficulty falling asleep, often talked in her sleep, and sometimes left her bed and walked about in a daze. The foster parents felt that L.S. suffered from feelings of intense rivalry and loneliness, seemed to be full of conflicts, and rejected everything and everybody.

L.S. entered a group residence at the age of 11½, after a pleasant camp experience. Her transfer to the group residence resulted from the foster father's request that she be removed from the home. Previous efforts at therapy had not been successful in maintaining her in the home and, at that time, she was placed in the hands of another therapist. It was constantly reported that she was a shy, anxious, distant, and uninvolved girl. To quote from her second therapist, "L.S. continues to be the same withdrawn, mistrusting, unhappy, constricted girl, with a tremendous problem in her relationship with males." She seemed to profit from the placement in the group residence, where she felt less threatened. The absence of the need for intense closeness in the milieu seemed to bring some relief to the situation.

She had made some minimal gains in therapy, despite her strong resistance. Nevertheless, she still appeared to be the same angry, constricted, suspicious, immature, easily frustrated, impulsive, phobic, and depressed preadolescent girl. Even when finally given what she wanted, she suddenly changed her mind and wanted no part of it.

By the time L.S. was 14, she was transferred to another group residence and by the time she was 15, she had become an excessive truant from school, absenting herself for 25 days during the year. The staff at the residence had been unable to get to the core of her behavior, except that she simply stated that she could not tolerate school. She had been placed in a cosmetology program, and the social worker suspected that there was some sexual identity confusion, perhaps some homosexual fears, stimulated by the program. The social worker had even raised the question whether the group residence program could reach L.S. or whether some other disposition should be made.

Since all the mental health work with L.S. had been placed in the hands of the social worker, a serious question had arisen about what could possibly be done by her to help L.S. make better use of her group residence placement and to help her make an external adjustment either to school or to some gainful employment. At the time L.S. was seen for the Separation Anxiety Test, she was working but there were many irregularities both in her attendance and her behavior.

Psychiatric Examination

According to the available record L.S. was seen four times for psychiatric study during a ten-year period. From the age of 6 to 9½ she had been interviewed three times by the same psychiatrist, who had followed her carefully from the time of the first clinic referral through the period of her early therapy. The three interview examinations, which were done during this period, showed very little change in diagnostic impressions. Generally, the diagnosis was "neurotic personality disturbance, mixed type with depressive and phobic features." When L.S. was first seen at the age of 6, the psychiatrist thought that an underlying psychotic disorder might be present. Later, when L.S. was 7½, the psychiatrist indicated a diagnosis of "neurotic personality disturbance with obsessive compulsive features" and observed some improvement. When L.S. was seen again at age 9½, although no diagnostic category was indicated, the psychiatrist stated that "In final analysis she appears to be a very troubled, depressed, severely phobic youngster, who more and more alienates herself from her families." It was at this time that the psychiatrist recommended psychotherapy, which was not begun until L.S. was 10½.

Even at age 6 L.S. had told the psychiatrist that she preferred to be alone and do things by herself. She felt that when she had been left alone and nobody bothered her, she could observe things better and enjoy them. Whenever her natural mother or her mother's paramour was discussed, she would become anxious and her facial expression, sad. At that time she had felt that something was wrong with her because she did not want to live with her mother. Her ambivalence concerning the need for the availability of the mother but her wish not to see her was patent. (From the vantage point of the author and from theoretical considerations, this problem may have been at the core of her personality disorder and was related to actual early separations as well as to threats of such separations). Even at that time she proved to have a poor attention span and appeared to be preoccupied, admitting to a great deal of daydreaming.

At 7½ L.S. showed a less rambling quality to her verbal productions, still admitted to daydreaming, and still loved to play by herself. At that time the psychiatrist felt that L.S. was profiting from a good foster home placement. He thought that overt rejection by her own mother and traumatic experiences with the mother and the paramour had created deep-seated conflicts in the child. At the time, the psychiatrist stated that despite noticeable improvement the girl was well on her way toward developing a neurotic personality structure with obsessive-compulsive features. The psychiatrist also noted that the girl had a rigid superego and ego structure, conformed excessively, and tried valiantly to please, and to avoid displeasing, others. It was the psychiatrist's impression that the child had an inordinate need to gain admiration, to be loved and accepted. She placed strong restraint on her emotions and concealed them from herself as well as from others.

The psychiatrist indicated that at age 9½ L.S. had become far less spontaneous than previously—cool, politely evasive, and guarded. Again the youngster indicated that "When you play alone you can do whatever you want" because "I don't like to give in to anybody." Yet, at the same time, she said that she got along with everyone "as long as they left her alone." At that time she reported having only one friend. She added that some friends are bad, because they promise everything and then do the opposite of what they promised. The girl told the psychiatrist that she suffered frequently from frightening dreams in which she was usually in an accident or train crash. She stated that even when she awoke, she could not get rid of the thought that she might be run over by a train or a car. In one of her dreams she fell on the tracks and a train ran over her. She saw herself in blood and said "I was chopped off."

The psychiatrist reported at that time that L.S. had very strong dependency needs, which remained unfulfilled either because she was not able to generate such a positive, warm reaction or because she was not able to receive it whenever it was offered. The increasing alienation was evident and in her dreams her destructive tendencies came out quite clearly. "She is yearning for protection, love and security. I am referring here, not only to emotional security and bodily self-preservation, but security of the personality as such, the quest of reality as a person in one's own right." The report stated further "This youngster has an almost obsessive need to scrutinize every person in her environment and their relationships with her. It seems the father figure is threatening and overwhelming and the mother figure rejecting and cold. The only positive person in her life is her sister. She appears to have basically rejected everyone else."

Shortly before her sixteenth birthday, L.S. was seen again by a psychiatrist because of her excessive truancy from school and because the group residence staff had difficulty reaching her. In summary, he made the following statement: "L.S. continues as before to present a somewhat depressed, avoidant, vague and guarded personality. She is either unable or unwilling to divulge much in the way of information as to what is happening to her internally. Diagnostically, rather than a definite statement, an impression is offered that L.S. remains a phobic, neurotic individual with depressive features who is distrustful of closeness, perhaps because of tremendous underlying need for dependency, attachment and gratification, the emergence of which or the acknowledgment of which is too threatening to her." The psychiatrist stated that a fuller diagnostic formulation was needed.

Her irregular school attendance appeared to be related to two factors: minimal effort in her work and difficulty in close relationships with other girls. (Note here the similarity to the attachment and individuation problems on the Separation Anxiety Test.) It was noted that verbally L.S. was underproductive, particularly with regard to a discussion of any emotionally charged areas. It was evident that she felt threatened about the possibility of being placed in a residential treatment center because of her behavior, and she wanted to avoid such placement at all costs. When her relationship with her teacher was discussed, L.S. became more uncomfortable and avoided and evaded the questions. However, it was elicited that L.S. had been fearful of her teacher's effort to get closer to her. At this point in the report the psychiatrist observed: "It appeared to this examiner that her judgment is limited and her capacity to be insightful and introspective is limited as well." (See results on the Separation Anxiety Test for correlative material.)

Psychological Examination

During the course of her stay with the agency, L.S. had been given three psychological examinations—the first when she was nearly 6, the second at the age of 9½, and the third when she was almost 14.

In her first examination she was recorded as of average intelligence, I.Q. 106, with a somewhat lower performance level. Her second examination indicated a bright normal level, I.Q. 115, with a performance level much lower—in the dull normal range. Her general level was considered to be average. When she was nearly 14, she was reported to have shown a steadily downward trend in intellectual functioning, Wechsler I.Q. Full Scale 87, with a relatively normal verbal level and a poor performance level. Generally, it appeared quite likely that she was of better than average intelligence but her psychomotor responses were generally poor.

In the earlier psychological examination it was found that on projective tests, the most significant theme was that of desertion and separation from family. Again it was emphasized that L.S.'s confusion and daydreaming arose out of her traumatic experiences,, the death of her father, the inability of the mother to take care of her and her siblings, and her moves from the mother's house to the grandmother's and then to the foster home.

At age 9½ she was seen as a more cooperative child, better organized but still producing in the Rorschach examination poorly conceived and loosely organized percepts. She definitely showed an increasing obsessive quality but also, at the same time, fragmentation with a loss of continuity. Thus, a number of her concepts were rather poor. At that time, however, despite her pleasantness, the psychologist found L.S. to be withdrawn and diffident, with little spontaneous conversation. It was felt that her anxiety and inattention immobilized her. There was considerable emphasis on her identity problem, whereas her general personality picture was flat, overconforming, and constricted, with a tendency to withdraw from meaningful and close interpersonal ties.

At age 14 L.S. was seen by a different psychologist, who stated that although L.S. was guarded and apparently rejected adults, she could relate to people in a childlike, dependent manner. She demanded nurturance but she displayed insatiable needs as well as guardedness, both of which precluded successful attainment of this goal. She seemed to see adults as unreliable purveyors of nurturance and turned to peers for fulfillment. Male figures, particularly, provoked phobic reactions and were also seen as potentially abandoning creatures. Although her reality testing was good, her judgment, particularly in social settings, was unreliable. The report indicated that she was quite unaware of her drive for obtaining nurturance. She needed people—and at this developmental stage boys—to give to her and to nurture a fragile self-concept. Without these, the underlying depressive trends came to the surface and L.S. had few other defenses to deal with the depression.

The latter psychologist diagnosed her as an immature, dependent young adolescent whose search for narcissistic gratification masked underlying depressive tendencies. L.S.'s investment in obtaining narcissistic gratification was seen as being in the process of crystallizing into her character structure. This left little motivational energy for intellectual and academic achievement.

Validation Conclusion

The picture of this girl's personality, as indicated on the Separation Anxiety Test, is, without doubt, highly correlative with her history, psychiatric interviews, and psychological tests. Throughout all the clinical material, certain characteristics stand out with considerable intensity. On the whole, throughout her life she related in a rather superficial manner toward other people, especially adults, with whom she was guarded and constricted. Although in periods of her life she appeared to be conforming, she showed evidence of difficulties in forming close relationships. This was demonstrated on the Separation Anxiety Test, in the attachment system in which she scored very low.

Another dominant characteristic which ran through all the material of her clinical history was the phobic response. This phenomenon, which ostensibly was related to the experience with the mother's paramour and the sexual traumatization therefrom as well as to the considerable difficulty in her relationship to adult male figures, was noted in the largest number of responses to the Separation Anxiety Test (8 out of the 44 responses were in the phobic area). All the diagnostic data in the psychological and psychiatric examinations had indicated a strong degree of phobic response, and a number of times the term "hysterical" had been inserted into her record. This was described in the Separation Anxiety Test analysis as a definite disorder of the fear-anxiety-pain system.

The disturbance of the defensive system was a similarly noteworthy finding in the test in which the reality avoidance and denial levels reached 23 percent and there was a strong emphasis on evasion. This characteristic had been found to be true in all her examinations and had been especially emphasized in the psychiatrics and in the periods of therapy. Denial and evasion had played important roles in frustrating her therapists' efforts in her behalf, and this was the second most dominant area on the Separation Anxiety Test.

A further correlative characteristic was seen in the poor judgment L.S. showed in discriminating between mild and strong separation stimuli. The element of poor judgment had been emphasized in many of the examinations and throughout her contacts with the caseworker. Moreover, her test results showed a very low individuation (self-reliance) level, an indication of poor self-sufficiency. Such a low level, especially in the presence of a poor attachment system response, indicated a girl of considerable dependency and needfulness, and at the same time with a poor capacity to return affection to an attachment figure. Throughout L.S.'s history this had been found to be a very serious failing in her character. This is a typical finding in a case of dependent detachment.

The lack of response to items in the areas of self-esteem preoccupation, self-love loss, and identity stress indicated a serious disorder of the self-evaluative system and can be described as a strong narcissistic orientation. This has continued to correlate with her self-involvement and schizoid behavior. Further, there was some suggestion that even in the psychosexual area, superficial relations with the opposite sex would probably obtain, and she would probably yield sexually on a dependency basis without receiving a really positive experience from it.

L.S.'s history demonstrated that gradually, over the years, her mistrust of people, her avoidance of closeness, her denial, her phobic responses, and her gradual loss of adequate adaptation to necessary schoolwork or even to employment requirements were integrally related to her neurotic character with depressive and phobic features and what has been referred to here as dependent detachment.

The Separation Anxiety Test clearly indicated that because of her limited personality makeup, insight therapy methods would be extremely difficult if not impossible. This had been demonstrated by the several unavailing and discouraging efforts at psychotherapy attempted over the years at the psychiatric clinic and in the residence, and was fairly obvious from the diagnostic impressions obtained during her psychiatric interviews. Despite these problems, efforts at therapeutic intervention and recommendations for such still continued to filter through into the reports of the various workers. The Separation Anxiety Test results finally convinced the staff of the abortive nature of this recommendation.

Another crucial diagnostic aspect of this case related to the degree of separation trauma L.S. had experienced. The frequency of her "yes" responses to the mental set questions on the Separation Anxiety Test was highly correlative with the entire history of the loss of supportive figures, all of whom represented very poor identification individuals to begin with. The only person in the family with whom this girl had any kind of identification pattern was her older sister, 10 years her senior, who in many ways had similar characteristics but who had apparently been a more successful adapter in terms of manipulative tactics.

It was recommended to the caseworker that L.S. required mainly strong management, in addition to highly reality-oriented interpretations of her behavior. The latter would be best used for narcissistic purposes rather than for insight. Clinical efforts in this case were considered to be of limited value, and prognostication for a good adjustment in the future was poor.

CASE 6 A.K., Male, aged 15½

An adolescent boy with a pseudopersonality pattern—a state of excessive self-sufficiency with strong aggressive reactivity. He circumvents separation pain by impulsive acting out.

Introduction

This case is an example of an adolescent youngster with an excessive self-sufficiency pattern. Such adolescents are encountered with a greater degree of frequency than Case 4 or Case 5. A.K. has a need for attachment, but this need is overshadowed by an excessive need to feel and act as though he is independent of such attachment. The high individuation (self-reliance) level on the Separation Anxiety Test is accompanied by considerable hostility. His aggression is often directed against authority figures and sometimes against peers when such peers are no longer useful for his manipulative purposes. In common psychiatric terminology he is seen as a character disorder.

A.K.'s affect is dominated by hostility, and pain is generally circumvented. The result is an aggressive acting out on an impulsive basis. His successes with people are accomplished on a manipulative and a psychopathic basis. A.K. makes use of people as objects for his own gratification, but he is sufficiently resourceful to have some successes in handling his environment. Dominating and controlling behavior have been part of his life style and he is often lacking in real basic feeling, especially for his peers. All is well with him as long as persons in his environment fit in with his particular drives and interests. It is also noteworthy that he tends to make a good impression on superficial acquaintance and he seems to be pleasant and well adjusted. This impression may last for quite some time, but he does not improve on further contact.

Sepatation Anxiety Test Results

A.K. came willingly to the examination and extended his hand in friendly greeting. It was noted that he did not leave his things in the waiting room but took everything with him to the examiner's office. He seated himself readily, offered no conversation, and waited to see what would occur. During the examination he showed no overt evidence of anxiety or disturbance. He conducted himself quietly and with poise and appeared to be generally quite self-contained. When he was asked later whether he was glad to be in a group residence with the agency, he smiled affably, saying that he was very happy with it.

A.K. approached the examination cautiously and deliberatively, thinking a good deal before giving his responses. A degree of wariness characterized his handling of the test items, but when he responded, he was definitive with very little indication of an insecurity about his responses.

He gave only 24 responses to the entire examination, which is a very low level of response. After completing the examination, he was asked to reexamine each picture to determine whether there were responses which he found acceptable. He added only two to the entire group. Constricted performances such as this are common in acting out character disorders. Two-thirds of his responses were to the strong pictures and one-third to the mild pictures, thus yielding a difference of 26 percent, which is within normal limits. Since three responses were the most he produced for any one picture, it could be said that his greatest responsiveness was to the following pictures: grandmother, judge, hospital, maternal death, and camp. The first four of these were all strong separation pictures, thus putting the camp picture among the strong stimuli, even though he had never been to a camp according to the "no" on the mental set questions. He gave only four "yes" answers to the mental set questions, thus indicating only a limited separation experience pattern. Yet he produced no responses at all to the sleep picture, merely commenting that the child in the picture feels tired. The material here appears contradictory, because he limited his responses on very mild pictures but reported few separation experiences. In view of his large number of adaptive, well-being, and sublimation responses, one would have to conclude that we were dealing with a characterological disorder.

An examination of the patterns of response indicated without question that we were dealing with a youngster with exaggerated self-sufficiency at the expense of normal separation pain reactions. A 50 percent individuation (self-reliance) was extraordinarily high and completely disporportionate to the other patterns or systems involved. Further, it should be noted that A.K. showed as many attachment responses as individuation responses on the strong pictures, which is also unusual. This exaggerated self-sufficiency reaction is commonly found in youngsters who strongly deny needful feelings. Nevertheless, he did show a 21 percent attachment reaction, which was within the normal range. What was abnormal was the complete absence of attachment reactions on the mild pictures, a phenomenon that strongly suggests repression of attachment need. Detachment appears to play some role in this boy's life, especially when separation threats are at a minimum.

The hostility percentage was at 17 percent, which is high and which, together with the very high individuation (self-reliance) percentage, clearly defined hostile acting out. The relative deactivation of the pain system in favor of the hostility system suggested that A.K.'s behavioral separation reactions would be either a general indifference—a loner status—or hostile acting out. As previously noted, individuals with this pattern handle their social relations on a superficial basis, do not generally form close ties, and are wary of closeness.

It seems likely that original bonding behavior was strongly traumatized by parental handling. Surrounded by a hostile environment, A.K. was forced to develop a strong reliance on his own capacity to deal with it.. According to the test patterning, he would handle his environment, not as a friendly one but as one likely to do him harm unless he was capable of manipulating

A.K. CHART FOR CONTROLLED ASSOCIATION RESPONSES

Picture Number	I	II	III	IV	V	VI	VII	VIII	IX	X	XI	XII	Total	Mild	Strong
Mental Set Response	N	Y	Y	Y	N	Y	Y	N	Y	N	Y	Y		2	2
Separation Intensity	S	M	M	M	M	S	M	S	M	S	S	S	4	2	2
Rejection	(2)	8	15	4*	13	10*	14*	11	15	11*	6	1	1	0	1
Impaired Concentration	17	11	11	1	6	4	11	15	16	17	16	15	0	0	0
Phobic Feeling	8	(2)	9	3	3	3	4	(6)	2	15	8	1'1	2	1	1
Anxiety	9*	16	1	2	11	5	13	12	12*	9	2	10	0	0	0
Loneliness	(5)	15	5	16	17	(9)	6	16	17	16	(15)	17	3	0	3
Withdrawal	3	12	8	13	7	12	8	7	3	4	9	14	0	0	0
Somatic	4	14	2	10	12	11	15	8	14	7	13	7	7	3	4
Adaptive Reaction	7	(7)	(13)	14	(14)	(15)	12	(4)	10	(8)	(11)	8	4	1	3
Anger	(11)	13	14	6	2	1	(5)	14	1	1	(5)	(2)	0	0	0
Projection	10	17	3*	17*	8	6	9*	1	6	14	10	6	1	0	1
Empathy	16	3*	12	9*	1*	13	1	5	13*	(10)	14	12*	0	0	0
Evasion	6	1	6	5*	10	14	16	9	4	5	7	4	1	0	1
Fantasy	14	10	7	15*	5*	17	3	2	9	(6)	12	9	2	1	1
Well-Being	1	9	4	8	(16)	2	17	(10*)	7	3	4	1	3	3	0
Sublimation	15*	5	(16)	(7)	(9)	7	10	13	11	12	17*	13	0	0	0
Intrapunitive	13	4	17	12*	15	16*	2*	3*	8	13	3*	3	0	0	0
Identity Stress	12	6	10	11	4	8	7	17	5*	2	1	16			
TOTAL	3	2	2	1	3	2	1	3	0	3	3	1	24	9	15

134

PATTERN SUMMARY CHART

RESPONSE PATTERN	Number of Responses		Total	% of Total Protocol	Area of Emphasis	Comment
	Mild II, III, IV, V, VII, IX	Strong I, VI, VIII, X, XI, XII				
Attachment (Sum of rejection, loneliness, and empathy)	0	5	5	21%	Loneliness	Norm but Spread A-typical
Individuation (Sum of adaptation, well-being, and sublimation)	7	5	12	50%	Adaptation	Very exaggerated abnormal emphasis
Hostility (Sum of anger, projection and intrapunitiveness)	1	3	4	17%	Anger	Strong but Emphasis O.K.
Painful Tension (Sum of phobic, anxiety, and somatic reactions)	1	1	2	8%	Phobic	Very low, Emphasis typical
Reality Avoidance (Sum of withdrawal, evasion, and fantasy)	0	1	1	4%	Fantasy and Fantasy	Very low, and Emphasis A-typical
Concentration Impairment and sublimation (Self-esteem preoccupation)	0:3	0:0	0:3	13%	Sublimation Impairment	Strong, and A-typical
Self-love Loss (Sum of rejection and intrapunitiveness)	0	1	1	4%	Rejection Intrapunitiveness	Very low
Identity Stress	0	0	0	0%	–	Very Low
Absurd Responses	0	1	1	–	–	Norm
Attachment-Individuation Balance	–	–	7	29%	–	Fair
Mild-Strong Scores & %	Score 9 37%	Score 15 63%	Diff. 6	Diff. 26%	–	Norm

it to his own needs. On the basis of the Separation Anxiety Test, A.K. often seemed friendly and related, but such behavior was not of any profound meaningfulness nor was it expected to last for any extended period. This is not to say that A.K. was incapable of feeling lonely, or of feeling rejected, or even of feeling empathy, but these feelings would be on a minimal level and not likely to dominate his intrapsychic life.

It seemed unlikely that A.K. would respond to close ties or that he would be interested in a therapeutic relationship. On the basis of the test he would be most likely to respond to milieu methods of relating. The trauma to his relatedness apparently left him unable to respond adequately to his adolescent regressive needs, a condition that produced a permanent state of immaturity. Therefore, he would be unlikely to permit himself full emotional release in a sexual situation, mostly because of his hostility and secondarily because of his unwillingness to permit himself to regress temporarily for fear that he may not be able to reestablish equilibrium.

Referral Problem

The supervising social worker of the Jewish Child Care Association had referred A.K. to the author for a Separation Anxiety Test because he thought that it would be interesting to study the recent effects of a separation experience. A.K. had recently been admitted to an agency group residence and some question had been raised as to how he would adapt to such a placement.

Background Material

A.K. was the only child of the mother's first marriage, which ended at the time that he was a year old. The mother felt that A.K.'s real father was unable to accept any responsibilities, and whenever he was unable to handle the situation, he would take off and go to an older brother. The father finally left the mother, appropriated all the money from their bank account, and never saw A.K. after he left nor did he make any effort to see him. The divorce came when the boy was 3 years old, the mother eventually went back to work, and A.K. was taken care of by a baby-sitter during this period. Finally, Mrs. K. remarried and had two more children, one when A.K. was 6 and another not too long before the referral.

According to the mother A.K. did fairly well in his development and showed few problems until the sixth grade in school, when he was reported having behavioral difficulties. When the second stepbrother was born, A.K. ran away after an argument with his mother and was apprehended in another state. While there, he stayed in the home of a policeman and A.K. talked of having this family adopt him. The mother began to see some of the same traits in the boy that she had seen in his father—for example, not assuming responsibilities and running away when he was faced with problems.

The mother had taken to reporting A.K.'s misbehavior to the stepfather, who was an extreme disciplinarian and who, sometimes, subjected the boy to physical abuse. The stepfather, a rigid, extremely angry man, felt the need to control his children without allowing them any individuality. He reported to the social worker that he had told his children what to do, when to study, and what their chores were, but otherwise had nothing to say to them.

The boy described himself as feeling like a vegetable at home, which he felt was an accurate description of his position in the house. The stepfather set very high academic standards for the youngsters and displayed many prejudices. On the other hand, the mother was considered to be a dependent, passive woman, who leaned heavily on her husband's strength. Generally, she would side with the stepfather and showed no regret over not having A.K. returned home after he ran away. Her attitude toward the boy was unrealistic but in a way different from that of the stepfather.

Further statements by the mother with regard to the boy's development were not especially noteworthy. She had not considered A.K. a problem as an infant; he ate and slept well. He was not toilet trained until he was 2½ because, although he understood, he would not cooperate. There was some suggestion that the mother's tolerance for negative behavior in a young child was limited and that she later appreciated the stepfather's rigidity as a form of strength she did not possess.

The social worker at Geller House, where A.K. had been placed after a brutal beating by his stepfather, suggested that the boy was more emotionally than physically abused. She believed strongly that he should be best placed in foster care, since he fantasized having a better home than his present one. It was the general feeling that a group home would be most appropriate. A.K. tended to feel superior to the youngsters at Geller House and consequently antagonized his peers. It was also considered desirable to refer him for individual psychotherapy.

Psychiatric Examination

The psychiatrist's major findings suggest that A.K. was hiding monumental rage. He had shown poor concentration and nervousness in school and had attributed this behavior directly to worry about going home to face what he had to face. Because he felt that he was a vegetable in his own home, he had run away. He wanted some kind of foster care, but he did not want to reside at a residential treatment center. He also described himself as having many friends and interests outside of the home, but because of abuse and the passivity of the mother, he did not enjoy anything any more. He could not recall daydreams, nightmares, or early memories, and in fact he became rather anxious when he was asked about them. He denied worries about himself and focused solely on the interactions between himself and his parents in the home. His ambitions were described as being largely in the field of law or law enforcement.

It was the psychiatrist's impression that A.K. was an ego-intact youngster without evidence of borderline pathology. He was considered to be a very ingratiating person, who attempted to minimize marked anger and sadistic fantasies through denial, projection, and rationalization. His anxiety could be attributed to marked defensive reactions to his own incipient outbursts of rage and sadism. He attempted to help himself in his association with adults at least by being ingratiating and condescending and using his verbal skills in a controlling manner. His self-portrayal was that of a mature, independent person, quite in control of himself.

There was evidence of marked exaggeration of the physical aspects of his relationship with his stepfather, and this extended into his fantasies about his real father. A.K. thought that his real father did not see him because he considered A.K. to be safe from harm, and the boy felt that his father was misinformed about this. He denied any positive or negative feelings with regard to this problem. It seemed relatively clear that his broadcasting of his own plight was an attempt in fantasy to reach the real father and be rescued by him, as well as an attempt to deny his sense of abandonment, disappointment, and subsequent anger. The possibility that A.K. would further provoke the stepfather was a matter to be considered. In the light of his very passive mother and abandonment by his real father, it was possible that a feminine identification might have occurred, that is, a feminine identification leading to provocative behavior and masochistic submission. However, there was no specific evidence of any sexual identity confusion at the time. The psychiatrist suggested a trial in a group home, along with outpatient psychotherapy.

Four months later, A.K. was seen by a psychiatrist at the Jewish Child Care Association. At that time he was showing serious provocative behavior and acting-out problems in the group residence to which he had been admitted. The psychiatrist suggested that A.K. may have been engaging in inappropriate, attention-seeking behavior and that this had begun to alarm the staff and many of the boys living there. For example, he climbed up on the ledge of a window, stole a parking meter, embarrassed the other boys by audacious behavior on a train and in a movie house, and when he was confronted with his action, he resorted either to denial or to rationalization in a seemingly affectless and detached manner.

Periodically, A.K. had arranged visits to various adults whom he described as close friends but who actually proved to be only acquaintances. He would often proclaim himself to others as being victimized by his family, espcially his stepfather. Again, the psychiatrist emphasized that A.K. exaggerated his mistreatment in his home. The psychiatrist noted that in the group residence he proved to be a difficult boy to relate to. When he was confronted with his failure to abide by rules, he offered weak excuses, such as not understanding the rules. He was argumentative, often with an omnipotent attitude. At times he made outlandish comments to the effect that he would commit suicide or that he was overwhelmed with worries, fears, and nervousness.

All these proved to be gross exaggerations or manipulative provocations. The staff at the residence observed that when he was caught off guard, he would be found laughing after making such comments. With time, he became more isolated from the other boys, who saw him as childish and annoying.

A.K. was also described as a short, immature-appearing adolescent, who spoke in a rapid and nervous manner. He came across as suspicious, evasive, manipulative, and controlling, and related primarily in a passive-aggressive manner. His guardedness and his readiness to deny and to rationalize when confronted suggested a conscious attempt to distort reality for immediate gain. In effect, he impressed the psychiatrist as being a verbal "con artist." There was also the suggestion of some expansiveness and even grandiosity in his thoughts and behavior. A.K. detailed at length a seemingly well-rehearsed story about his stepfather's mistreatment of him and he repeated much of what he had told the previous psychiatrist. When he was confronted with his exaggerated accusations or with his acting-out behavior, he reacted with a progression of denials leading to rationalizations and eventually to a kind of weak admission of previous behavior, which he insisted no longer obtained.

His affect tended to be labile and there was a suggestion of impulsiveness and excitability devoid of depth of feeling. Object relations were largely superficial interactions dominated by manipulations to obtain immediate gratifications. Avoidance and evasion were frequent defensive maneuvers.

The psychiatrist at the Jewish Child Care Association made a diagnosis of "behavior disorder of adolescence with mixed paranoid and passive-aggressive personality traits." There was no evidence of psychotic thinking. Further, the psychiatrist stated: "I believe that he should be treated as an adolescent whose acting-out behavior stems mostly from his ingrained characterological problems. As such, it is important to set up clear-cut expectations for him and to be prepared to challenge his need to test out these rules." The psychiatrist added that although A.K. pretended that he was liberated from any restraints or limits, he was, in fact, not prepared at this time to leave the safety of placement. It was the general feeling that he would ultimately respond to structure, firm limits and frequent confrontation. At this time no recommendation was made for therapeutic intervention.

Parenthetically, in corroboration with psychiatric opinion, the caseworker in the group residence pointed out that the boy was so well defended and out of touch with his own feelings that he often presented what he had to say with no affect.

Psychological Examination

This examination had been administered at Geller House. The psychologist described him as of average intelligence (Wechsler I.Q, 101). His performance, though relatively consistent, ranged from average to superior levels. The psychologist stated that the boy's anxiety and general immaturity seemed to prevent the use of his ability in a consistent fashion. His strengths included his superior verbal abstraction, his above-average vocabulary, and his above-average common sense and reasoning. His visual-motor functioning was also considered above average.

Using a number of projective tests including the Rorschach, Bender-Gestalt, House-Tree-Person, and Thematic Apperception Tests, the psychologist concluded that A.K. was an insecure, anxious youth who was preoccupied with themes of damage, injury, and mutilation. He was basically an immature, frightened boy who had difficulty in viewing his experiences or his environment in other than these terms. There was considerable variability in ego functioning but with adequacy in assessing and testing reality. His percepts were accurate and detailed and showed some ability to be imaginative. Although he generally thought in global rather than in detailed terms, he showed himself able to recognize and deal in specifics.

It was in the area of dealing with impulses, however, that he experienced most difficulty. Basically, he had problems in recognizing his impulses and he typically handled these either by repression or by projection. Nonetheless, he experienced considerable tension because of the damming up of his instincts. There was considerable difficulty in the normal expression of aggressive impulses, of which he often attempted to remain unconsciously unaware. However, his percepts on ink blots often indicated feelings of damage. It was the general impression that the boy was struggling with internal, seething anger, which remained unexpressed. His high degree of tension and anxiety suggested that the defenses he utilized were only marginally successful.

There was evidence in certain portions of the projective tests that A.K. had experienced an intense feeling of loss of his natural father. It was the psychologist's impression that A.K. was attempting to achieve closeness with his stepfather and was frustrated and disappointed in his inability to do so. It was concluded that the boy felt the need for an available male with whom he could empathize and identify. The psychologist spoke of A.K. as being "fixated at an anal level." This was inferred from his compliance and submissiveness. On one level it reflected his passivity; on another it represented anal retentive orientation. It was further concluded that he related to others in a fashion which satisfied them rather than his own needs. Other people's acceptance of him was very important, and he was likely to go to great lengths to win the approval of others. At the same time, there was a masochistic orientation, possibly representing his attempts to find acceptance as well as to fend off his sadistic impulses. He was generally seen as moving in the direction of an obsessive-compulsive personality with masochistic features, and the psychologist felt that he was in need of intensive treatment.

Validation Conclusion

There was a considerable difference of opinion between the interpretation of the Separation Anxiety Test and the psychologist's test impressions, but the test seemed to correlate well with the background material and the most recent psychiatric report. The emphasis in the Separation Anxiety Test was on the extreme self-sufficiency and the strong hostility, although there was evidence of capacity for attachment. However, the latter was completely overshadowed by a need to deny the need for others. All the professional workers had agreed with this impression, but there was no evidence of a more masochistic trend in the Separation Anxiety Test. The greatest emphasis seemed to be on A.K.'s externalization of his hostility and his denial. The notion that this boy had a great deal of anxiety, as described by the psychologist, is not borne out by the Separation Anxiety Test or by the psychiatric examination. The picture seen by both the JCCA psychiatrist and by the Separation Anxiety Test was that of a characterological disorder rather than the obsessive-compulsive pattern interpreted by the psychologist. There was total agreement that A.K. was not psychotic, but contrary to the psychologist's report there seemed to be no evidence that this boy had any deep feelings of rejection or intrapunitiveness. It appeared that he circumvented many of the typical feelings of more sensitive individuals and reacted more with immediate aggression and hostility than with emotional pain.

It was also of interest that in the Separation Anxiety Test A.K. did not react to the denial patterns. With this kind of self-sufficiency pattern, what we really saw was a denial of denial; that is, he denied that he was not telling the truth. This would be similar to what the JCCA psychiatrist meant when he reported that the boy denied that he was not telling the truth or that he was exaggerating. Further, this is what the social worker was referring to in his report that the boy did not appear to feel any overt anxiety and that exaggeration was a more immediate and natural response for him. It was the author's interpretation that the lack of response to the attachment system on any of the mild pictures was an indication of the boy's lack of profound interest in an attachment relationship. It seemed that only strong separation situations would induce this boy to seek out a protective figure. But it was obvious that it would be necessary for him to display bravado, as shown by his equal attachment and individuation responses to the strong pictures. This test result correlated with the observations of the social worker and the counselors in the group residence, as well as with remarks made by the psychiatrist.

This case fits the description of the "false self" discussed by Winnicott. There has obviously been considerable deactivation of several important psychological systems, including the fear-anxiety-pain system, as well as aspects of the attachment system and a tremendous exaggeration of the individuation (self-reliance) system. Effects of separation on the self-evaluative system were denied, a serious failing in any personality experiencing separation. This deactivation of systems strongly supports the contention of excessive self-sufficiency and of a characterological disorder.

CASE 7   E.W., Male, aged 13, and Family Study

> *An adolescent boy with hostile anxious attach-*
> *ment in a strong family attachment system dom-*
> *inated by hostility and mutually destructive be-*
> *havior. The case is also an illustration of the use*
> *of the Separation Anxiety Test on each member*
> *of the family of a youngster referred for residen-*
> *tial placement.*

Introduction

This case is an example of how the Separation Anxiety Test can be used to study the nature of the attachment relationship between a boy and other members of his family. Even though there was a great deal of disturbance in the relationships among the family members, it demonstrates how a highly attached youngster, despite a good individuation score, can be filled with anger, evasion, and withdrawal, and can feel strongly rejected when faced with a separation situation. It illustrates further how an entire family can show some strong similarities in attachment need, especially in the area of loneliness and unhappiness, in the face of separation experiences. It shows how strong currents of anger and resentment can permeate a family in which there was in operation a symbiotic system that in some ways was destructive of the welfare of the parents as well as of the children. It seemed likely in this case that the symbiotic system might well interfere with any placement plans for this boy. It may be helpful to study this case as an example of how an entire family can be evaluated through the use of the Separation Anxiety Test.

The Separation Anxiety Test results for all members of this family are presented in the order in which the tests were given. Each test is anlyzed separately, and a family summary is then attempted. All the tests on this family were given personally by the author at the Jewish Child Care Association.

Separation Anxiety Test Results—E.W.

E.W. came to the examination in a very solemn and angry mood. Although he acceded to being examined, he did so in a resigned fashion. He rarely looked straight at the examiner, keeping his face averted most of the time, except when looking at the pictures in the test. Considering his behavior and his attitude, it was surprising that he was so responsive and that he went through the examination without complaining.

He gave a total of 59 responses, which is within the average range. However, the difference between his responses to the mild pictures and the strong pictures was much more than usual and indicated a hypersensitivity to the strong pictures. In and of itself, this suggested considerable sensitivity to any strong separation experience. There were 7 out of 12 pictures in which he responded "yes" to the mental set questions as to whether or not he had had the experiences depicted. This was slightly above the average and included "yes" responses to the pictures of the argument between the father and the mother, with the father leaving the house and the mother leaving for the hospital. (As will be noted later, both of these events actually occurred.) There were more responses to the items of loneliness than there were to any other type of response to the pictures. Further, on the picture of the mother leaving the sleeping child, he produced responses of fear and loneliness, which are not typical of a boy of his age level. Accompanying the loneliness response were four other dominant responses: rejection, withdrawal, anger, and adaptation. These responses proved to be very useful in understanding this boy's problem.

The balance between attachment and individuation was a very good one, and there were no abnormalities in this patterned relationship. Moreover, the strength indicated by the summation of these factors suggested ego intactness, which has been referred to as core strength. Nevertheless, this is counterbalanced by the degree of hostility on the strong separation pictures. At the same time, separation pain was below the norms, suggesting that to some degree pain is circumvented in favor of hostility. Furthermore, the defensive system was above the norms and was dominated by withdrawal and evasion. Such a pattern is associated with hostile acting out.

E.W. CHART FOR CONTROLLED ASSOCIATION RESPONSES

Picture Number	I	II	III	IV	V	VI	VII	VIII	IX	X	XI	XII	Total	Mild	Strong
Mental Set Response	N	Y	Y	Y	Y	Y	N	N	Y	Y	N	Y	7	5	2
Separation Intensity	S	M	M	M	M	S	M	S	M	S	S	S			
Rejection	2	8	(15)	4*	13	10*	14*	(11)	15	(11)*	(6)	(5)	5	1	4
Impaired Concentration	(17)	11	11	1	6	(4)	11	15	16	(17)	16	15	3	0	3
Phobic Feeling	8	2	9	3	(3)	3	4	(6)	(2)	15	8	11	3	2	1
Anxiety	9*	16	(1)	2	11	5	13	(12)	12*	9	2	(10)	3	1	2
Loneliness	(5)	15	(5)	16	17	(9)	6	(16)	(17)	16	(15)	(17)	7	2	5
Withdrawal	(3)	12	8	(13)	(7)	12	8	7	3	(4)	(9)	14	5	2	3
Somatic	4	14	(2)	10	12	11	15	(8)	14	7	13	7	2	1	1
Adaptive Reaction	(7)	(7)	13	(14)	(14)	(1)	(12)	4	10	8	11	8	5	3	2
Anger	11	13	14	6	(2)	(1)	5	(14)	1	1	(5)	(2)	5	1	4
Projection	10	17	3*	17*	8	(6)	9*	(1)	6	14	10	6	2	0	2
Empathy	16	3*	12	9*	1*	(13)	(1)	5	13*	(10)	(14)	12*	4	1	3
Evasion	(6)	1	6	5*	10	14	16	9	4	5	(7)	(4)	3	0	3
Fantasy	(14)	10	7	15*	5*	17	3	2	9	6	12	9	1	0	1
Well-Being	1	(9)	4	(8)	(16)	2	10*	10*	7	3	4	(1)	4	3	1
Sublimation	15*	5	(16)	(7)	9	7	10	13	(11)	12	17*	13	3	3	0
Intrapunitive	13	4	17	12*	15	16*	2*	(3*)	8	13	3*	(3)	2	0	2
Identity Stress	(12)	6	10	11	4	8	7	17	5*	2	(1)	16	2	0	2
TOTAL	7	2	5	4	5	5	2	8	3	4	7	7	59	20	39

E.W.
PATTERN SUMMARY CHART

RESPONSE PATTERN	Number of Responses		Total	% of Total Protocol	Area of Emphasis	Comment
	Mild II, III, IV, V, VII, IX	Strong I, VI, VIII, X, XI, XII				
Attachment (Sum of rejection loneliness, and empathy)	4	12	16	27%	Loneliness	Excessive but Emphasis typical
Individuation (Sum of adaptation, well-being, and sublimation)	9	3	12	20%	Adaptation	Strong
Hostility (Sum of anger, projection and intrapunitiveness)	1	8	9	15%	Anger	Strong
Painful Tension (Sum of phobic, anxiety, and somatic reactions)	4	4	8	13½	Phobic and Anxiety	Norm but Emphasis A-typical
Reality Avoidance (Sum of withdrawal, evasion, and fantasy)	2	7	9	15%	Withdrawal and Evasion	Strong but Emphasis A-typical
Concentration Impairment and sublimation (Self-esteem preoccupation)	0:3	3:0	3:3	10%	None	Typical
Self-love Loss (Sum of rejection and intrapunitiveness)	1	6	7	12%	Rejection	Strong
Identity Stress	0	2	2	3%	–	Weak
Absurd Responses	1	1	2	–	–	Norm
Attachment-Individuation Balance	–	–	32	54%	–	Excessive
Mild-Strong Scores & %	Score 20 34%	Score 39 66%	Diff. 19	Diff. 32%	–	Strong

147

Damage to the self-evaluative system was evident in the frequency of the feeling of rejection response and the high level of the self-love loss pattern. Even on a mild picture, such as the neighborhood moving picture, this distress in the self-evaluative system appeared. It is justifiable to suggest that in a separation situation, even when it is mild, E.W. would respond with a low level of self-evaluation. A weak identity stress response added to this picture.

In summary, E.W. responds to the Separation Anxiety Test with considerable inner strength, but nevertheless with strong hostility, feelings of rejection, weakness of the self-evaluative system, withdrawal, and acting out. Dynamically, this behavior represents considerable unmet or unassuaged needfulness, thus resulting in a malformation of the character structure and producing an angry, acting-out youngster. It is obvious from the pattern of rejection responses that his acting out is self-defeating. In view of this problem, we can understand the reason why his identity stress percentage was so low as to indicate immaturity in his ability to handle the usual needs for change in adolescence. It seemed likely from the test patterning that sooner or later this boy would have to undergo psychotherapy or face the possibility of having to leave his home for a more structured type of treatment.

Separation Anxiety Test Results—N.W. (Sister)

Directly after the testing of E.W., his sister, N.W., aged 11-10, was examined. She appeared to be pleasant, smiling, and cooperative throughout the examination. She did not display any disturbance or distress and seemed content to deal with the test requirements.

N.W.'s responsiveness was limited to 38 answers, which is below the norms and therefore a constricted pattern. Like her brother, she showed a very large difference between the number of mild and strong responses, suggesting considerable sensitivity to separation experiences. Also like her brother, she produced 7 affirmative reactions to the mental set questions and she also emphasized the loneliness response.

N.W.'s sensitivity to separation was strongly demonstrated in the areas of preoccupation with self-esteem and intellectual operations, but she also demonstrated a high attachment reaction. Her self-evaluative system seemed more intact than her brother's, but there was a similar weakness in the identity stress area. She also showed a strong personality core, as indicated by the strength in both the attachment and the exploratory (self-reliance or individuation) systems. However, she did not indicate strong hostility, and the fear-anxiety-pain system was much stronger than her brother's. From this patterning there seemed to be an indication of a more normal overt reaction to separation. The exceptions appear in the emphases in some of the patterns, an overemphasis on sublimation while underplaying adaptation, and an overemphasis on anxiety rather than overt fear. The defensive system seems to be typical and relatively intact. Evasion is not emphasized in N.W.'s record, as it was in her brother's.

N.W. was far more willing to admit separation pain than was her brother. Although she did select some rejection responses, these were far fewer than her brother's and her self-love loss pattern was not so extensive as that of E.W.'s. There was also evidence of difficulty in transferring attachment need from family members to peers and other adults.

The test profile indicated that N.W. was less needful than her brother, and on the sleep picture she simply selected a sublimation response. She gave a rather interesting response to the picture of the brother going away on a voyage, stating: "Maybe I feel happy that my brother is going where he wants to, that he's grown up and soon I'll be able to grow up and do it too."

In summary, N.W. responded to the Separation Anxiety Test as a far more constricted person than her brother, although just as attached and just as strong in personality. She showed stronger drives for sublimation, a better self-evaluative system, and a much better capacity to express emotional pain. She had obviously adopted a different and perhaps a better personality adjustment than her brother, but still was needful in a number of areas. Apparently, she had to make certain sacrifices in this family in order to maintain this adjustment.

Picture Number	I	II	III	IV	V	VI	VII	VIII	IX	X	XI	XII	Total	Mild	Strong
Mental Set Response	N	Y	Y	Y	Y	Y	N	N	Y	Y	N	Y	7	5	2
Separation Intensity	S	M	M	M	M	S	M	S	M	S	S	S			
Rejection	(2)	8	15	4*	13	10*	14*	11	15	11*	6	(5)	2	0	2
Impaired Concentration	(17)	11	11	1	6	(4)	11	15	16	(17)	16	15	3	0	3
Phobic Feeling	8	2	9	3	(3)	3	4	6	2	15	(8)	11	2	1	1
Anxiety	9*	16	1	2	11	5	13	(12)	12*	(9)	(2)	10	3	0	3
Loneliness	(5)	15	5	16	(17)	(9)	6	16	17	(16)	(15)	17	5	1	4
Withdrawal	3	12	8	13	(7)	12	8	7	3	4	(9)	(14)	3	1	2
Somatic	4	14	2	10	12	11	15	8	14	(7)	13	7	1	0	1
Adaptive Reaction	7	(7)	(13)	14	14	15	12	4	10	8	11	8	2	2	0
Anger	(11)	13	14	6	2	1	5	(14)	1	1	5	(2)	3	0	3
Projection	10	17	3*	17*	8	6	9*	(1)	6	14	10	6	1	0	1
Empathy	16	3*	12	9*	1*	(13)	1	5	13*	(10)	(14)	12*	3	0	3
Evasion	6	1	6	5*	10	14	16	(9)	4	5	7	4	1	0	1
Fantasy	(14)	10	7	15*	5*	17	3	2	9	6	12	9	1	0	1
Well-Being	1	9	4	8	16	2	(17)	10*	7	3	4	1	1	1	0
Sublimation	15*	(5)	(16)	(7)	9	7	10	13	(11)	12	17*	13	4	4	0
Intrapunitive	13	4	17	12*	15	16*	2*	(3)*	8	13	3*	3	1	0	1
Identity Stress	12	6	10	11	4	(8)	7	17	5*	2	1	(16)	2	0	2
TOTAL	5	2	2	1	3	4	1	5	1	5	5	4	38	10	28

PATTERN SUMMARY CHART

RESPONSE PATTERN	Number of Responses		Total	% of Total Protocol	Area of Emphasis	Comment
	Mild II, III, IV, V, VII, IX	Strong I, VI, VIII, X, XI, XII				
Attachment (Sum of rejection, loneliness, and empathy)	1	9	10	26%	Loneliness	Strong but Typical emphasis
Individuation (Sum of adaptation, well-being, and sublimation)	7	0	7	18%	Sublimation	Norm but Abnormal emphasis
Hostility (Sum of anger, projection and intrapunitiveness)	0	5	5	13%	Anger	Norm
Painful Tension (Sum of phobic, anxiety, and somatic reactions)	1	5	6	16%	Anxiety	Strong but Emphasis A-typical
Reality Avoidance (Sum of withdrawal, evasion, and fantasy)	1	4	5	13%	Withdrawal	Norm
Concentration Impairment and sublimation (Self-esteem preoccupation)	0:4	3:0	7	18%	Sublimation	Very strong
Self-love Loss (Sum of rejection and intrapunitiveness)	0	3	3	8%	Rejection	Low
Identity Stress	0	2	2	5%	–	Low
Absurd Responses	0	1	1	–	–	Norm
Attachment-Individuation Balance	–	–	33	87%	–	Very High
Mild-Strong Scores & %	Score 10 26%	Score 28 74%	Diff. 18	Diff. 48%	–	Very High

Separation Anxiety Test Results—L.W. (Mother)

The mother, a schoolteacher, aged 36, came to the examination just as readily as her children. Her cooperation was good, although she had very little to offer spontaneously during the course of the examination. It was noted that she tended to be ambivalent and reacted with some confusion and insecurity. It should be understood that in administering the test to an adult it is necessary to ask the person to identify with the child in the picture, having in mind her (his) own childhood. This alteration of instructions is essential in order that the reactions to the pictures relate to the mother (father) rather than to her (his) child.

The mother admitted to 6 out of the 12 affirmatives on the mental set questions, gave 54 responses, which is within the average range and, as did her children, produced a far larger percentage of difference between the strong and mild pictures than the norms. Thus, all was well so long as separations were mild, but strong separations produced severe intensity of response. As with her children, she gave the largest number of responses to the loneliness item. Her second largest number of responses were to rejection and anxiety, which are, of course, highly diagnostic in relation to her personality. The similarity to her son in the rejection response was fairly clear. Of considerable importance was the dominance of the intrapunitive response in the hostility area, which was opposite to that of her son, whose record emphasized anger. From this it seemed that he produced anger and that she absorbed it intrapunitively.

The mother's record indicated far more disturbance than any other member of the family. Like her children, the mother indicated that she was a highly needful person and expressed the highest percentage of attachment need. However, there was some weakness in the individuation system as the frequency of responses in this area dropped below the norms and represented approximately only half of the attachment responses. The weakness was demonstrated first by the equality of individuation responses on the mild and strong pictures and secondly by the nearly equal attachment and individuation responses on the mild pictures. This is a symbiotic indicator and suggests serious problems in coping with separations.

Strong separation affect was demonstrated, because 34 percent of her responses were in the areas of separation pain and separation hostility, which were both equal in intensity. The hostility pattern was even stronger than her son's and contained strong intrapunitive as well as projection responses. Separation pain was dominated by anxiety and, in frequency, was similar to her daughter's. This is not a typical reaction on this test and is more commonly seen in individuals with poorly controlled anxiety. Separation denial was very strong and quite high, with limited responsiveness in the withdrawal area. This excessive defensive system suggested an intrapsychic evasiveness, which is often seen in seriously disturbed persons. Along with this the self-evaluative system indicated damage, as shown by the strong loss of self-love, which included both rejection and intrapunitive responses. This pattern boded ill for L.W.'s sense of adequacy.

The above patterns, which include strong attachment, weak individuation, high level of affect, strong separation denial, high levels of self-love loss, and weak identity stress, are a characteristic of severe anxious attachment and self-destructiveness. Such persons, under the internal fear of abandonment, tend to become either depressed, suicidal, or both. Since the number of absurd responses was within normal limits, it was unlikely that L.W. was psychotic. Nevertheless, her level of disturbance suggested serious problems in emotional control, a high degree of needfulness expressed in feelings of rejection, and a tendency to become overwhelmed by the stresses of life. It seemed likely that she would constantly border on difficulties in coping with life's demands, and strong separation experiences would be quite devastating for her. Being a highly attached, emotional woman, she could easily be destroyed by her own needfulness. Her intrapsychic efforts to escape from the significance of a strong separation indicated that her denial of such problems could sometimes take on delusional forms.

It became quite evident from this examination that the mother was definitely in need of psychotherapy and that, should the boy be placed, intensive treatment would be needed over a long

L.W. (MOTHER OF E.W.) CHART FOR CONTROLLED ASSOCIATION RESPONSES

Picture Number	I	II	III	IV	V	VI	VII	VIII	IX	X	XI	XII	Total	Mild	Strong
Mental Set Response	N	Y	Y	Y	Y	Y	Y	N	N	Y	Y	N	6	3	3
Separation Intensity	S	M	M	M	M	S	M	S	M	S	S	S	6	3	3
Rejection	(2)	8	15	4*	13	(10)*	14*	(1)	15	11*	(6)	(5)	5	1	4
Impaired Concentration	(17)	11	(11)	1	6	4	11	15	16	17	16	15	2	1	1
Phobic Feeling	8	2	9	3	3	(3)	(4)	6	2	15	(8)	11	3	1	2
Anxiety	9*	16	(1)	2	11	(5)	13	(12)	12*	(9)	(2)	10	5	1	4
Loneliness	(5)	15	5	16	17	(9)	6	(16)	(17)	(16)	(15)	10	7	1	6
Withdrawal	3	12	8	(13)	7	12	8	7	3	4	9	(17)	1	1	0
Somatic	4	14	2	10	12	11	15	8	14	(7)	13	7	1	0	1
Adaptive Reaction	7	7	13	14	(14)	(15)	12	4	(10)	(8)	11	8	4	2	2
Anger	(11)	13	(14)	6	2	1	5	14	1	1	5	2	2	1	1
Projection	10	17	3*	17*	8	(6)	9*	1	6	(14)	(10)	6	3	0	3
Empathy	16	3*	12	9*	1*	(13)	(1)	5	13*	(10)	14	12*	3	1	2
Evasion	(6)	1	(6)	5*	10	14	16	(9)	4	5	7	(4)	4	1	3
Fantasy	14	10	(7)	15*	5*	17	3	(2)	9	(6)	(12)	9	4	1	3
Well-Being	1	(9)	4	8	(16)	2	17	10*	7	3	4	1	2	2	0
Sublimation	15*	5	16	(7)	9	7	10	13	11	12	17*	13	1	1	0
Intrapunitive	(13)	4	17	12*	15	16*	2*	(3)*	8	13	(3)*	(3)	4	0	4
Identity Stress	12	6	(10)	11	4	8	7	(17)	5*	2	(1)	16	3	1	2
TOTAL	6	1	6	2	2	7	2	7	2	7	8	4	54	16	38

154

L.W. (MOTHER OF E.W.)
PATTERN SUMMARY CHART

RESPONSE PATTERN	Number of Responses		Total	% of Total Protocol	Area of Emphasis	Comment
	Mild II, III, IV, V, VII, IX	Strong I, VI, VIII, X, XI, XII				
Attachment (Sum of rejection loneliness, and empathy)	3	12	15	28%	Loneliness	Very strong but Typical emphasis
Individuation (Sum of adaptation, well-being, and sublimation)	4	4	8	15%	Adaptation	Weak but Typical emphasis
Hostility (Sum of anger, projection and intrapunitiveness)	1	8	9	17%	Intrapunitive and projection	Strong with Abnormal emphasis
Painful Tension (Sum of phobic, anxiety, and somatic reactions)	2	7	9	17%	Anxiety	Strong but Abnormal Emphasis
Reality Avoidance (Sum of withdrawal, evasion, and fantasy)	3	6	9	17%	Evasion and Fantasy	Strong with Abnormal emphasis
Concentration Impairment and sublimation (Self-esteem preoccupation)	1:1	1:0	2:1	5%	Concentration Impairment	Low and A-typical emphasis
Self-love Loss (Sum of rejection and intrapunitiveness)	1	8	9	17%	Rejection	Very strong and Abnormal
Identity Stress	1	2	3	5%	–	Weak
Absurd Responses	0	3	3	–	–	Norm
Attachment-Individuation Balance	–	–	25	46%	–	Norm
Mild-Strong Scores & %	Score 16 30%	Score 38 70%	Diff. 22	Diff. 40%	–	Very High

period. There was no doubt that the separation process would be very difficult for the mother, possibly more so than for her son. The mother was a very important part of the symbiotic system in this family, and although she was having many difficulties with her son and despite the strong hostile interaction between the two, there was a deep attachment between them. With her strong symbiotic pull, she would obviously have considerable ambivalence about placing the boy. Such ambivalence is often seen in cases of severe anxious attachment as well as severe hostile-anxious attachment.

Separation Anxiety Test Results—A.W. (Father)

The father, aged 48, was a small man, who several times broke appointments before coming in for the test. When he finally arrived for the test, he appeared to be apprehensive, serious faced, and concerned. Although he cooperated on the test, it was obvious that he was as deliberative as the mother in handling the selection of the various items.

He admitted to only 5 of the 12 separation experiences on the mental set questions, the lowest score of any other member of the family. Both children had admitted to 7, and the mother, to 6. Like the other members of the family, the father had an unusually small number of responses to the mild pictures in comparison to the strong ones, but the difference percentage between the two was higher than that of any of the others. This suggested that A.W.'s sensitivity to separation was even stronger than that of any of the others. Despite this, he produced only 42 responses, which is a constricted record and is similar to the daughter's. The largest proportion of his responses in the test was to the item of loneliness, but in his case no other response was near this level in frequency. Further, and quite important, he did not select any of the adaptive responses (making the best of the situation). This is very unusual and is strongly symptomatic of a highly dependent person whose suffering from separation would cause serious adjustment problems.

The above statement is borne out by a study of the patterns of the test. A.W.'s attachment percentage of 29 was the highest in the family, and he gave more attachment than individuation responses on the mild pictures. This is a symbiotic indicator. The conclusion is further verified by the total absence of indivduation responses on the strong pictures. His total individuation percentage was 5 percent, an extremely low figure. At the same time he produced an extraordinarily high separation pain reaction of 26 percent, with only a 7 percent hostility pattern—a total affect level of 33 percent. Like other members of the family, he presented a strong defensive system, which was evidence of weakness in dealing with reality problems. He did not react with high levels of self-love loss or self-esteem preoccupation, which, as seen later, did not accord with the reality of his situation. The low emphasis on separation hostility suggests that A.W. would accumulate feelings of resentment until such time as he could not bear it any longer.

The total protocol was characteristic of strong anxious attachment with a symbiotic factor. The father was obviously a highly attached and needful individual, with an extremely high level of separation anxiety and a strong inability to accept separation. He was weak, highly dependent, lonely, and obviously not a person who should be living alone. From this test it appeared likely that the father was the most dominantly symbiotic individual in the family and strongly anxiously attached. Being the most dependent, he would have serious separation problems but these would be of a somewhat different nature than the mother's. Since at the time I saw him, I had learned that he had been separated from his wife, it became obvious from the test that this experience must have been extremely painful for him.

Separation Anxiety Test Results—Family Summary

An examination of the family patterns on the Separation Anxiety Test indicated that there was a profound attachment between the members of this family, despite the separation between the parents and the amount of hostility that permeated the various relationships in their interaction. Psychologically, this family was not really able to separate in a normal fashion, and had a disturbed attachment system. The nature of the attachment appeared to be filled with destructive emotion, a need for hostile interaction, as well as a high general level of anxiety for anxiety-producing stimuli. On the mother's part, a strong self destructive trend was

A.W. (FATHER OF E.W.)   CHART FOR CONTROLLED ASSOCIATION RESPONSES

Picture Number	I	II	III	IV	V	VI	VII	VIII	IX	X	XI	XII	Total	Mild	Strong
Mental Set Response	N	N	N	Y	Y	Y	N	N	Y	Y	N	N	5	3	2
Separation Intensity	S	M	M	M	M	S	M	S	M	S	S	S	S		
Rejection	②	8	15	4*	13	10*	14*	⑪	15	11*	6	5	2	0	2
Impaired Concentration	⑰	11	11	1	6	④	11	15	16	17	16	15	2	0	2
Phobic Feeling	8	2	9	③	3	3	④	⑥	②	15	⑧	11	5	3	2
Anxiety	9*	16	1	2	11	⑤	13	⑫	12*	⑨	②	10	4	0	4
Loneliness	⑤	⑮	5	16	17	⑨	6	⑯	⑰	⑯	⑮	⑰	8	2	6
Withdrawal	③	12	8	⑬	7	12	8	7	3	4	9	⑭	3	1	2
Somatic	4	14	2	10	12	11	15	⑧	14	7	⑬	7	2	0	2
Adaptive Reaction	7	7	13	14	14	15	12	4	10	8	11	8	0	0	0
Anger	⑪	13	14	6	2	1	5	⑭	1	1	5	②	3	0	3
Projection	10	17	3*	17*	8	6	9*	1	6	14	10	6	0	0	0
Empathy	16	3*	12	9*	1*	13	①	5	13*	⑩	14	12*	2	1	1
Evasion	⑥	1	6	5*	10	14	16	9	4	5	7	④	2	0	2
Fantasy	14	10	7	15*	5*	17	3	②	9	6	⑫	9	2	0	2
Well-Being	1	9	4	8	⑯	2	17	10*	7	3	4	1	1	1	0
Sublimation	15*	5	16	7	⑨	7	10	13	11	12	17*	13	1	1	0
Intrapunitive	13	4	17	12*	15	16*	2*	3*	8	13	3*	3	0	0	0
Identity Stress	⑫	6	⑩	11	4	8	7	⑰	5*	②	①	16	5	1	4
TOTAL	7	1	1	2	2	3	2	8	2	4	6	4	42	10	32

158

A.W. (FATHER OF E.W.)
PATTERN SUMMARY CHART

RESPONSE PATTERN	Number of Responses		Total	% of Total Protocol	Area of Emphasis	Comment
	Mild II, III, IV, V, VII, IX	Strong I, VI, VIII, X, XI, XII				
Attachment (Sum of rejection, loneliness, and empathy)	3	9	12	29%	Loneliness	Excessive but Typical emphasis
Individuation (Sum of adaptation, well-being, and sublimation)	2	0	2	5%	Well-Being and Sublimation	Very weak and Abnormal emphasis
Hostility (Sum of anger, projection and intrapunitiveness)	0	3	3	7%	Anger	Very low but Typical emphasis
Painful Tension (Sum of phobic, anxiety, and somatic reactions)	3	8	11	26%	Phobic	Excessive but Typical Emphasis
Reality Avoidance (Sum of withdrawal, evasion, and fantasy)	1	6	7	17%	Withdrawal	Very strong but Typical emphasis
Concentration Impairment and sublimation (Self-esteem preoccupation)	0:1	2:0	2:1	7%	Concentration Impairment	Low
Self-love Loss (Sum of rejection and intrapunitiveness)	0	2	2	15%	Rejection	Low
Identity Stress	1	4	5	12%	–	Very strong
Absurd Responses	0	0	0	–	–	Norm
Attachment-Individuation Balance	–	–	27	64%	–	Too High
Mild-Strong Scores & %	Score 10 24%	Score 32 76%	Diff. 22	Diff. 52%	–	Too High

159

observed. The material suggested that both parents came to their marriage immature, dependent, and highly needful, and it was obvious that they were not in any position to give to their children a capacity for normal development. It was plain that the boy had developed a strong sadomasochistic need in his interactions with the family, and that his sister had made certain character sacrifices in order to achieve an adjustment to the family situation. The father, being a weak and inadequate individual, obviously was not in any position to act as an adequate model for the boy.

The tests suggested that the mother was in dire need of help of one kind and the father was strongly in need of help of another kind. The mother's coping mechanisms were marginal, and a serious separation event could throw her into an emotional crisis with possible suicidal implications. The latter is derived from the fact that her pattern summary was very similar to that of suicidal youngsters previously studied (Hansburg, 1976). It seemed likely that separating the boy from his mother would be necessary in order to reduce the sadomasochistic interaction and to aid the boy to a healthier approach toward human relationships. In view of his intense dependency and symbiotic problems, it became obvious that the father was a person in great need of understanding and affection and would find it difficult to make an adequate life for himself.

Since all the above inferences were derived directly from the Separation Anxiety Tests of the entire family, in line with the question of validation it is of interest to determine the degree to which the material obtained from the family history as well as from other clinical sources correlated with these diagnostic and dynamic formulations of the tests.

Referral Problem

E.W. had been in treatment for a number of years but he had not been able to involve himself in the treatment process. He continued to have behavior problems at home as well as at school and was extremely abusive and violent toward the mother, who was afraid of losing her controls. E.W. was very strong willed and, for the most part, did what he wanted. He had been apprehended for truancy as well as smoking in the school bathroom. He was unmanageable at home and he refused to involve himself in psychotherapy. The father indicated that the boy had taken money from him but the boy denied that he had.

Background Material

The social worker interviewed all the members of the family. She reported that E.W. was a sullen-looking, heavyset boy who would neither make eye contact with her or allow himself to become engaged in the interview in any meaningful way. When the family entered the office, he first refused to remain in the same room with his father and his sister. He threatened to leave and finally agreed to stay only if his mother were present. All attempts to involve him even in casual conversation were met with hostile sounds. When his mother pleadingly begged him to cooperate, he would push her away angrily and at the same time started to cry. It was clear that the boy was enraged with his mother and the social worker for forcing him to confront the possibility of placement as a reality, and his rage equaled his fear and unhappiness about such a possibility. The only verbal reaction the social worker was able to get from the boy was a volley of abusive epithets and then stony silence.

Both parents reported that E.W. had had school adjustment problems from the very beginning. He first attended a private school and then a public school from which he was expelled, and was presently doing better in a private academy. He was reported to have always been an explosive boy with poor impulse control and to have been very aggressive and destructive at home. He literally broke up whatever was in front of him. He had physically assaulted his mother and his sister, but he was also capable of being reasonable, attentive, and affectionate toward his mother. His behavior was generally unpredictable and it was difficult to foretell what might provoke him. In spite of such behavior, he had many friends and had been invited to many parties, which he apparently enjoyed.

The sister, on the other hand, was an attractive girl who had a much more open manner than her brother. She was glad to involve herself in the interview and, while recognizing that it would be difficult for the boy to go away, nonetheless felt that it was hard for the family to live with him. She also showed a marked negative attitude toward her father, often talking disparagingly to him and about him. N.W. had also shown some problems of her own. She was caught shoplifting and was considered to be an emotional girl. She did not want to face problems; she would either wish them away by covering up her feelings or simply by sleeping them off. As the main target for the boy's rage, she felt that the parents did more for E.W. than for her. The social worker suspected that the girl tended to direct her anger toward herself rather than toward others.

The mother was seen as a petite woman, with a somewhat pinched face, who wore glasses. She was poorly dressed and gave the impression of neglecting her personal appearance. She was obviously a very bright, articulate, and assertive person, who struggled to keep herself under control. She was very concerned about her children, particularly about E.W. She had sufficient insight into the family pathology to recognize that therapeutic intervention was urgently needed by her son. Nevertheless, she was very ambivalent about placement for the boy and was visibly disturbed about the decision she had to make. She looked back wistfully at the boy's early years and recalled the pleasure he had been to her. Her vision of the past was filled with reminiscences of the lost opportunities in her handling of him, and these thoughts were painful to her.

The mother herself had grown up in a very intense household. Her father was a very rigid, unreasonable, and punitive person. She had experienced physical abuse from her father and both she and her mother were afraid of him. The father was a truck driver, who had gambled away his money, and the family experienced long periods of economic deprivation. She remembered being brutally punished, a memory that made her unable to punish her own children. The pattern of uncontrollable rage had been widespread in her family; her paternal uncle had been accused of killing a man in a fight. Her own son's uncontrolled assaultiveness (he once threatened the mother with a knife) raised questions in the mother's mind as to her own homicidal feelings toward him. She feared that there might be a congential inferiority in her family.

The social worker noted that the father was a stocky, short man, who wore a toupee. He had a weak face, and failure seemed to be written all over him. Like his wife, he was very bright and verbal. He also presented himself as very concerned about his children and as trying desperately to be a part of their lives. The children, however, showed little interest in being with him.

The father described his own mother as a cold, bossy, and domineering person. He had feared her all his life and had tried in vain to please her. He described his own father as a passive, unassertive person, who would fall apart under pressure. The latter was reported to have worked in a garment factory, and his mother had managed the finances of the family. The father's family had always lived very frugally and they had accumulated considerable savings. This was in contrast to the mother's family. The father, who was an attorney, had a younger brother who was very successful in the legal profession, but the brothers saw very little of each other. The father felt that his brother could have helped him professionally but had not done so. The father had a limited legal practice and minimal income.

The social worker viewed both parents as emotionally deprived, each seeking from the other the support he or she could not give. The father, who was much older than his wife, perpetuated in their marriage the verbal and physical abusiveness that the mother had experienced from her own father. The turbulent family life led the family to seek help at a family service agency, but aid was discontinued because of their inability to modify their behavior. A number of years later the family sought help at a mental health center and remained for several years. The mother viewed her marriage as a bad one, and the only stable period in her life was during her pregnancy.

Several years prior to this referral the mother had made a serious suicidal attempt (see suggestive pattern in the Separation Anxiety Test) and was hospitalized. After this event, the mother separated from the father and went into psychotherapy with a psychiatrist. Subsequently, the parents obtained a divorce. The father remained in therapy with another doctor. The boy was to have been in therapy with a third doctor but he refused treatment.

Psychiatric Interview

E.W.'s resistance to revealing current feelings characterized the psychiatric interview. Nevertheless, he did attend the session despite his initial opposition, which was understandable in view of his association between the interview and the projected placement. He talked with the psychiatrist to the very end of the session, at which time he flew into a rage and left the office. This blowup was precipitated by the psychiatrist's recommendation that he enter into placement.

During the examination the examiner noted that E.W. was a heavy-set, somewhat casually dressed adolescent, who looked his stated age. His mood and attitude toward the examiner was one of barely controlled sullenness and disdain beneath an ingrained guardedness. He was, unquestionably, an angry boy filled with suspicions and expectations of annoying intrusions on his life and freedom. Although he initially spoke rather freely, he rigidly defended himself against any kind of probing or confrontation. He openly announced his refusal to answer certain questions, and became visibly annoyed when his wishes were not immediately accepted. Throughout, there was a quality of superiority and disdain in his reactions, which broke through sporadically in angry outbursts. At one point his resentment mounted in response to questions regarding what situations aroused his temper. He blurted out "When people ask stupid questions!" Although his affect was dominated by tense, angry feelings with an underlying explosive potential, it was appropriate to thought content. His thinking processes were organized, logical, and adequately reality oriented. Accordingly, there was no evidence of a definite psychotic process (a similar conclusion in the Separation Anxiety Test). There was, however, a tendency to resort to denial and externalization of blame (similarly in the Separation Anxiety Test). His fantasies revealed some expansiveness and insatiable need.

In terms of dynamics, the most significant psychiatric finding was the presence of marked separation anxiety, apparently related to a symbiotic attachment to the mother (again see results of the Separation Anxiety Tests). In any case this boy had great difficulty in separating from the mother and would resort to desperate maneuvers to reestablish contact. For example, during a recent summer, on the second day at camp he called home in tears, begging his mother to take him home. He eventually managed to get home after ten days by pretending that he was to attend his grandparents' fiftieth wedding anniversary party. Before that, when his parents denied his plea to return from camp, he deliberately cut his hand. Recently, his response to a discussion by his parents regarding placement was to break a chair against the wall. Evidently the boy was terrified of being separated from the mother through placement, and he feared that this time his parents would carry through their threat. He seemed capable of the most extreme manipulations to bolster his insistence on remaining home. The psychiatrist was impressed most of all by these facts, some of which he obtained from the interview, some from the social worker, and others he inferred.

It is interesting that the psychiatrist made a diagnosis of a "behavior disorder of childhood, with mixed aggressive and passive traits and considerable explosive potential." The nature of the intense anxiety and anger in relation to the attachment to the mother did not appear as part of the diagnosis but appeared in the addenda. Thus the psychiatrist stated that of most significance at this time was E.W.'s marked separation anxiety aroused by the recent procedures of placement, which had threatened to disrupt his symbiotic relationship with his mother. The psychiatrist added further that E.W. was a stubborn, controlling, angry boy who was likely to resort to desperate measures to avoid separation. It was thought that he needed placement to provide optimal conditions for further growth and individuation. The psychiatrist concluded with the following note: "Unfortunately, I don't know if this boy could accept placement long enough to effect a change in this symbiotic attachment."

Psychological Examination

E.W. displayed behavior similar to the above during the psychological examination. He obtained a verbal I.Q. of 126, a performance I.Q. of 131 and a total I.Q. of 131. This classified him as of very superior general intelligence. Four years earlier he had obtained I.Q.'s of approximately 20 points higher than these. On the current examination he showed marked instability in intellectual functioning, failing many simple test items and passing more difficult ones. The psychologist referred to the bases of this instability first as disruptive tension and second as self-indulgence. E.W. seemed to do better when he showed less need for personal interaction in a verbal way, as demonstrated by his handling of the performance test portion of the examination. When he encountered new tasks, he tended to become blocked, but was able to persevere and to complete tasks. He showed good capacity for planning, organizing, and integrating. Although at the time of examination E.W. had completed only the seventh grade, his arithmetic level was grade 10.7 and his reading level measured at 11.3. Obviously, his achievement in school skills was equivalent to his intellectual capacity.

Projective tests implied that E.W. was an impulsively acting and tension-ridden adolescent who was struggling to repress much inner depression and anxiety. He attempted to maintain his defenses through sterotypy and evasion. Under emotional stress, he clung to the very concrete and the stereotyped. His associations reflected the severely defensive facade that he had been maintaining. He presented highly varied passive-aggressive tensions, which would be expected on a developmental basis. The psychologist further theorized that the boy utilized aggressiveness in order to counteract a strong tendency toward passivity.

The psychologist was impressed by the differences between the boy's surface appearance of social and emotional withdrawal and the underlying expenditure of energy to sustain his repression of anxiety. Following this line, the examiner concluded that the boy acted out and thus avoided anxiety. His hostility, cynicism, and defiance were considered to be protection against the conscious recognition of his security needs.

The examiner further interpreted the tests as suggesting that E.W.'s aggressiveness reinforced his immaturity. Although he showed aspirations which he could achieve intellectually, he could not follow through behaviorally. Thus he remained highly frustrated. An additional interpretation was that the aggression was also turned inward and resulted in depression. Although on the surface E.W. was hostile to the females in his family, he yearned for support and security from them. He could be both masochistic and sadistic in his compelling need to cling to the security of the home. He experienced his father as compatible but also as ineffectual; the female he experienced as much more dominant. As a result, he seemed to have some confusion of sex-role attributes.

The psychologist finalized his report with the statement that E.W. had severe, unresolved passive-aggressive tensions, which received double reinforcement from both adolescent development and his family situation. It was suggested that the boy could benefit from a stable and supportive residential treatment center.

Validation Conclusion

The purpose of this case study had been to determine whether the Separation Anxiety Test, when administered to all members of a family, would give some insight into the nature of the interaction and would provide significant clues as to personality factors in each family member. It was posited theoretically that there is a system which maintains the members of a family in an orbital relationship to one another. Tentatively, we have been using the term symbiotic system to characterize this particular family's interaction. Since the Separation Anxiety Test reveals so readily the nature and extent of attachment as aroused by threats of separations, the kind of defenses used to maintain it, and the degree of strength in the individuation process, it seemed to us that the test would lend itself readily to an understanding of this system.

The most startling corroboration was seen in the degree of attachment need present in each member of this family, with the probability that the father was the most symbiotically needful. Although the attachment was strong, the maintenance of this system appeared to have been accomplished largely through aggressive manipulation and hostile interaction. It was fairly clear that the boy's demandingness toward the weak and symbiotically needful parents could not be gratified. This was demonstrated in the history, the Separation Anxiety Test, and the clinical study of the boy.

Strong corroboration was most noteworthy between the psychiatric interview and the Separation Anxiety Test results. In both that interview and the test, the kind of defenses used by E.W.

against external invasions of his relationships with the family were highly corroborative, as was seen by the extent of the test's separation denial pattern and its implied defensive system. The highly individualistic nature of the boy's approach to situations was demonstrated on the psychological examination, in the psychiatric interview, and in the Separation Anxiety Test. Although there were some differences in how the boy's patterned responses were interpreted by the various clinicians, they generally agreed that the aggression dominated the pain as an expressive phenomenon in E.W., a characteristic commonly seen in passive-aggressive personalities. There was further agreement concerning the depressive syndrome referred to by the psychologist and in the damage to the self-evaluative system referred to in the interpretation of the Separation Anxiety Test. The combination of hostile acting out and a depressive syndrome was generally found in all the observations of the boy. The extent of the boy's personality strengths appeared in the clinical evaluations, which all agreed represented the absence of any psychosis.

The Separation Anxiety Test appeared to have been very sensitive to the parental personality structures. Thus, for example, the instability of the mother was revealed quite clearly in the test, and a striking corroboration of her suicidal potential was seen both in the test and in her past history. She had demonstrated on the Separation Anxiety Test all six of the known self-destructive factors and, as can be seen from the record, she had attempted suicide several years before. A weakness in the individuation level was shown in both parents, strikingly in the father. The father was seen as a weak, dependent individual driven by anxiety and fear of loss of a symbiotic figure. Whereas the mother showed a most severe anxious attachment pattern, the father produced a strong anxious attachment pattern. These patterns in the parents appear to have been reflected mainly in the acting out and in the boy's depressive feelings rather than in a symbiotic pattern in the boy's test.

In the members of this family, feelings of rejection were significant. The backgrounds of both parents showed much disturbance and neither of them manifested adequate personality preparation for parenthood. In this connection the needfulness was definitively demonstrated in the Separation Anxiety Test results. The tests indicated that both parents were in need of treatment; of course, the background material gave evidence that both parents were already in treatment and had been for a long time.

The parents' fear of parting with the boy, even though his behavior demonstrated that placement was necessary at this point and was so recommended by the staff, was traceable to the patterns described above. In the postcritical period of this study, it was largely the father who started the resistance against placement of the boy and who finally succeeded in convincing his wife and the agency that placement would not be good for his son. This he accomplished by enlisting the aid of his sister, a former social worker. Both parents then withdrew the boy from further contact with the agency. This move was a further indication that the father had the most dominant symbiotic influence in the family precisely because he himself was a weak, dependent person. He was able to swing the mother to his opinion because of her ambivalence and her own emotional disturbance. The mother had shown a much higher level of individuation than the father, but her own capacity for dominating and controlling the family affected other aspects of their lives.

The place of the sister in this family was also revealed by the tests. Although she too was an attachment-oriented person, she showed a somewhat reasonably good individuation level. There was an indication that she had made certain sacrifices in adapting to this family; these were in relation to characterological deviations. This fact was indicated not only by the Separation Anxiety Test but also by the reports of symptomatology she had shown in the previous few years.

It would appear that we learned much more about this boy and his interaction within the family by administering the test to all members of the family than if we had given the test to him alone. The tests provided us with valid predictions of subsequent behavior and helped us understand significant personality characteristics of each member of the family. Studies of other families with this test instrument have since proved to be of considerable value in child placement work.

CASE 8   R.F., Male, aged 15½

An adolescent displaying hostile detachment. This case is a combination of organic brain dysfunction, superficial self-sufficiency, difficulty in forming meaningful attachments, considerable projected hostility, and serious weakness in judgment.

Introduction

This case is an example of an organically brain-damaged youngster with considerable variations in intellectual functioning and in whom evidence of emotional traumatization is obviously demonstrated on the Separation Anxiety Test and is highly correlated with the history. In this case a great deal of anger which is easily projected and a great deal of superficial self-sufficiency represented the dominant characteristics, especially on the Separation Anxiety Test. In all situations in which this boy had lived, it was demonstrated that he had difficulty in forming meaningful and close attachments of a lasting nature, whether with his parents, foster parents, institutional settings, therapists, and others.

The case also illustrates serious weaknesses in judgment, in sense of identity, and in the ability to accept and deal with separation experiences without serious problems of withdrawal and evasion. Thus, it is an interesting case in which a disorder of the character structure is superimposed on a basic organic brain dysfunction.

The case also illustrates the type of problem in which the objectives of any therapeutic efforts would have to be limited and in which insight would have a minimal role. As demonstrated both by the Separation Anxiety Test and by the history, this boy would have serious acting-out problems which would be disturbing to all individuals with whom he associated, especially adults and authority figures.

Separation Anxiety Test Results

R.F. was given the Separation Anxiety Test at the age of 15½ by Dr. Martin Vigdor of the Psychiatric Clinic at the Jewish Child Care Association. The test was given during a program of a full psychological battery with the hope that it would reveal the boy's attitude toward separation from parental figures and would further elucidate his problems and his personality. Throughout the examination R.F. behaved in an annoyed, irritated manner and desperately tried to end the procedure. He was very aggressive in his responses on the test.

R.F. produced a total of 83 responses to the Separation Anxiety Test, of which 40 responses were on the mild pictures and 43 on the strong pictures. Although these results indicate a very responsive record, there was an obviously poor differentiation between the mild and strong stimuli. This reaction was largely a result of the responses to the class transfer and the neighborhood move pictures, which are considered mild pictures and which produced more responses than any of the strong pictures.This would suggest that these pictures were highly traumatic for R.F., which is quite unusual in a test that contains pictures of a far higher level of separation stimulation. A reaction of this type is most often seen in persons with poor judgment in their general behavior and in their human relationships.

The test items R.F. referred to most frequently were adaptation and anger, on which he had 9 responses each. The large number of responses to these two categories immediately suggested the dominance of angry acting out and excessive self-sufficiency when contrasted to loneliness and to fear or anxiety. The next most dominant reaction was somatic pain, which is unusual in a record of this kind. Further, an interesting response was the small number of affirmative answers to the mental set questions, which is characteristic of youngsters who have experienced few separations from home. (As noted later, the history demonstrated that this boy had had a very large number of separations, some of which occurred early in his life and were quite traumatic.) Therefore, it seemed likely that R.F. was not telling the truth in his responses to these questions or had forgotten much of his past life.

The important pattern percentages in the Pattern Summary Chart are the below-normal attachment level, the high individuation level, and the very high degree of hostility. While a superficial self-sufficiency is present, the most significant pattern is the enormous percentage of hostility (23 percent), which is the

R.F. CHART FOR CONTROLLED ASSOCIATION RESPONSES

Picture Number	I	II	III	IV	V	VI	VII	VIII	IX	X	XI	XII	Total	Mild	Strong
Mental Set Response	NN	NN	YY	YN	YNN	YN	NN	NN	N	N	NN	NNY	4	3	1
Separation Intensity	S	M	M	M	M	S	M	S	M	S	S	S			
Rejection	2	(8)	(15)	4*	13	10*	14*	(11)	15	11*	6	5	3	2	1
Impaired Concentration	17	(11)	(11)	1	6	4	11	15	16	17	16	15	2	2	0
Phobic Feeling	8	(2)	9	3	3	3	4	6	2	15	8	(11)	2	1	1
Anxiety	9*	16	(1)	2	11	5	13	12	12*	(9)	(2)	10	3	1	2
Loneliness	5	(15)	5	16	17	(9)	(6)	(16)	17	(16)	(15)	(17)	7	2	5
Withdrawal	(3)	(12)	8	(13)	(7)	12	8	7	(3)	4	(9)	(14)	7	4	3
Somatic	4	(14)	(2)	10	(12)	11	(13)	8	(14)	(7)	(13)	(7)	8	5	3
Adaptive Reaction	(7)	(7)	(13)	(14)	14	15	(12)	(4)	(10)	8	(11)	(8)	9	5	4
Anger	(11)	13	(14)	(6)	2	(1)	(5)	(14)	1	(1)	(5)	(2)	9	3	6
Projection	(10)	17	(3*)	17*	(8)	6	9*	(1)	6	(14)	10	(6)	6	2	4
Empathy	16	3*	12	9*	1*	(13)	(1)	5	13*	8	7	12*	4	1	3
Evasion	6	(1)	6	5*	10	(14)	16	(9)	4	5	12	4	3	1	2
Fantasy	14	10	7	15*	5*	(17)	3	2	9	(6)	4	9	2	0	2
Well-Being	1	9	(4)	(8)	(16)	2	17	(10*)	7	3	1	1	4	3	1
Sublimation	15*	5	(16)	(7)	9	(7)	10	13	(11)	12	17*	13	4	3	1
Intrapunitive	(13)	(4)	17	(12*)	15	16*	2*	3*	8	13	3*	(3)	4	2	2
Identity Stress	(12)	6	10	(11)	(4)	(8)	(7)	17	5*	(2)	1	16	6	3	3
TOTAL	6	9	9	7	5	7	6	7	4	8	7	8	83	40	43

172

R.F.
PATTERN SUMMARY CHART

RESPONSE PATTERN	Number of Responses		Total	% of Total Protocol	Area of Emphasis	Comment
	Mild II, III, IV, V, VII, IX	Strong I, VI, VIII, X, XI, XII				
Attachment (Sum of rejection loneliness, and empathy)	5	9	14	17%	Loneliness	Weak but Typical emphasis
Individuation (Sum of adaptation, well-being, and sublimation)	11	6	17	20%	Adaptation	Strong but Typical emphasis
Hostility (Sum of anger, projection and intrapunitiveness)	7	12	19	23%	Anger	Excessive but Typical emphasis
Painful Tension (Sum of phobic, anxiety, and somatic reactions)	7	6	13	16%	Somatic	Norm but Abnormal Emphasis
Reality Avoidance (Sum of withdrawal, evasion, and fantasy)	5	7	12	14%	Withdrawal	Strong but Typical emphasis
Concentration Impairment and sublimation (Self-esteem preoccupation)	2:3	0:1	2:4	7%	Sublimation	Low
Self-love Loss (Sum of rejection and intrapunitiveness)	4	3	7	8%	Intrapunitive	Norm but Abnormal to Self-Esteem
Identity Stress	3	3	6	7%	–	Weak
Absurd Responses	2	1	3	–	–	Norm
Attachment-Individuation Balance	–	–	15	18%	–	Weak
Mild-Strong Scores & %	Score 40 48%	Score 43 52%	Diff. 3	Diff. 4%	–	Very Low

173

highest of all the patterns on the test. The combination of hostility responses, although dominated by anger, also contained an excessive number of projection responses, which suggests a strong paranoid flavor to the hostility. Projection responses occurred on some of the mild as well as the strong separation pictures, and one of these was an absurd reaction. Since the hostility pattern was higher than the attachment pattern, the interpretation places this boy in the dangerous and highly impulsive category. This conclusion is derived largely from the fact that there would not be enough attachment to act as a stabilizing force against the boy's demonstration of hostile feeling projected outwardly. A pattern of this kind is defintely pathological, and R.F. would be consdered as potentially homicidal. As noted in Hansburg (1972, no. 1), uncontrolled separation hostility represents a serious danger.

As previously noted, somatic reactions dominated the separation pain area and were considered not only unusual but also pathological. In view of the degree of deactivation of the attachment system, these somatic reactions must be considered as an indigenous problem. (Note discussion of organicity in background material and medical findings.) R.F. is apparently aware of physical problems.Of additional significance is the reduction of separation pain responses from the mild to the strong pictures—an abnormal patterning. Combined with the separation hostility pattern,this pattern is often associated with individuals who have developed delinquent trends and in whom anxiety is gradually denied in favor of hostile, externalized behavior.

The level of separation denial or reality avoidance was somewhat higher than expected and was dominated by withdrawal and evasion, with fantasy having the smaller number of responses. This kind of pattern is more often seen in character disorders than in the normal population. It is interesting that R.F.'s relative indifference to such a severe situation as being placed by the court and as shown in the judge picture (the boy included an evasion response in this picture) is an indication of how far he had gone, not only in excessive self-sufficiency, but also in denying the effect of severe separations. This behavior is in line with the denial that appeared in his responses to the mental set questions.

Evidence of a depressive factor appeared in R.F.'s selection of items dealing with the self-evaluative system. Here the self-love loss area was slightly stronger than the preoccupation with mental functioning. This is a characteristically depressive factor (Hansburg, 1976) and indicates damage to the self-evaluative system.

In summary, the results of the Separation Anxiety Test suggested that R.F. had a severe character disorder dominated by hostile, aggressive acting out with an excessive self-sufficiency pattern, paranoid attitudes, somatic preoccupation, and a damaged self-evaluative system. This case has been classified as one of hostile detachment with elements of paranoid masochism. From the results it appeared unlikely that insight forms of therapy would be useful in this case and that placement in a controlled setting would have to be considered.

Referral Problem

When R.F. was 15½ years old, he was referred by the Post Placement Unit of the Jewish Child Care Association which had been providing casework service for him and his family since he had returned from his Pleasantville Cottage School Placement 15 months prior to referral. He was considered to be "continually angry, sullen, and defiant" and his adjustment at home, school, and the community had been poor. He showed a pattern of poor judgment and impulsiveness, had frequent altercations with his family, and stole from them. Because of truancy from school and possession of marijuana, the court was involved in his case and his mother had filed a PINS petition against him. The major concern at this point was that R.F.'s acting-out behavior would take a turn for the worse. The request for evaluation came in connection with a referral of R.F.'s case to the Joint Planning Service of the above agency with the question of replacing him in a residential treatment center.

Background Material

R.F. was the product of an incompatible and unsatisfactory marriage. The mother had married at the age of 19 because it was the thing to do and all her friends had already been married. Her own parents had objected to the marriage because they considered the husband to be inferior to their daughter. The mother did not recall evidences of love and affection toward her husband, nor was there any physical attraction, although she reported that he was "nice and considerate" to her despite her obesity, and she appreciated this attention. The first six years of their marriage were ostensibly compatible because she worked days and he worked nights and therefore both had little opportunity to communicate. They saw each other only on Sundays, which the father spent sleeping. The mother eventually realized that she and her husband had little in common, because she was interested in art, the theater, reading, and other cultural pursuits; the father's interests were T.V. and comic books. Sex relations were often not satisfactory—the father was passive and the mother, aggressive.

When R.F. was 1 year old, the mother asked the father for a legal separation and agreed to a temporary separation for a period. During one of the father's visits, the mother asked for a divorce. This request enraged the husband, and in a partially intoxicated condition, she submitted to him sexually and became pregnant. She was extremely upset and anxious when she discovered her unplanned pregnancy at a time when she had taken steps for a legal separation. She hoped and prayed for a miscarriage, which did not materialize. Another child was born, a boy, and the mother suffered a postpartum depression, which she was able to overcome with medication. She had only contempt for and anger toward the father, and three months after the second child's birth, she became involved with a married man. When R.F.'s father became aware of this, he asked for a divorce and moved out of the house. This was a shock to the mother, despite all previous alienation and disagreements.

Eventually, the mother decided to place her two boys in a private foster home, return to her parents, and accept a job so that she could support the boys. The mother maintained constant contact with the foster parents and visited the boys regularly. The foster parents were described by her as an elderly non-Jewish couple who seemed understanding and kind to both children. By the time R.F. was 8 years old, the father instituted a custody suit. After a court hearing, during which the boys, the foster parents, and the mother, as well as the father and his new wife, testified, the custody of both boys was awarded to the mother, with the stipulation that she provide a home for the boys. Since then, R.F. and his brother and mother lived together in a cooperative apartment. A very friendly relationship had been maintained with the foster parents, and the boys visited them occasionally. At the time that R.F. was seen by the Jewish Community Services Agency, he seemed outgoing and friendly but immature in his behavior.

Previous to R.F.'s conception, the mother had two miscarriages as well as an atopic pregnancy, for which she had undergone surgery. After a full-term 9-month pregnancy, R.F. was delivered by natural labor and with no anesthetics. The baby had developed colic and cried a good deal, and despite the mother's consultations with various physicians regarding his condition, she received little help. After 6 months, the colic improved and eventually the baby's feeding was on a more normal schedule. R.F. was remembered as a very active baby, who seemed to be in constant motion. He walked at 8 months and also sat up early. When the baby was in the play pen, he never sat still, but always walked around and tired quickly of any toys. There were problems regarding toilet training and bowel training and R.F. was enuretic until the age of 7, although he did have occasional accidents after that time. The mother mentioned the possibility of hereditary bladder weakness, because she too, as well as her brother, were enuretic until the age of 13.

The boy showed no unusual behavior when he was a toddler, except that he was always extremely overactive. At the age of 9, he seemed to lack confidence and sometimes, under tension, he stuttered. He was generally considered to be immature, although he enjoyed sports, especially ball playing, bowling, and swimming. At that age it was suggested that R.F. remain in therapy at a clinic, pending resolution of placement planning, since it appeared to be antitherapeutic to involve the child with treatment that might have to be interrupted by placement.

R.F. was referred to the Joint Planning Service of the Jewish Child Care Association and was subsequently placed at the Pleasantville Cottage School He was given a thorough examination by a neurologist and was found to be suffering from organic brain damage. It was apparent at the time that the boy could not function in a regular school and was placed in a special school. Finally, it was decided that his acting-out behavior—for example, lighting a fire at the urging of other children and an incident involving a knife and showing off its use—precipitated placement. Thus, at the age of 10, he was placed in the Pleasantville Cottage School, where he was considered to be dependent, immature, hyperactive, and somewhat difficult to manage. At the time, it was obvious to those who had contact with him and his mother that the mother was not supplying this boy's great need for attention and he was diagnosed as having "a behavior disorder of childhood with unsocialized aggressive reaction." It was stated that the established organic dysfunction of the central nervous system rendered him more vulnerable to the mother's emotional distance, postpartum depression, the parents' separation, and his subsequent placement.

R.F.'s adjustment to the Pleasantville Cottage School improved considerably in the first year. He was generally well behaved in the cottage and showed no major problems. On trips he often took responsibility for the other boys because he did not want the trips ruined by problems among them. He was fond of athletics and of his friends in the field. It was noted that when he was sitting in the cottage, his thumb was often in his mouth, and that when he was tired, he slept all curled up in the fetal position. He was closer to the female cottage parent than to the male, often wanting to sit in her room. He was quite nonverbal, talking mostly only when he had something to boast about. It was commented at the the time that R.F. needed much nurturing and steady support; the question was, how much could the mother offer?

At intake, the mother was completely uninvolved and clearly didn't feel much like a mother. As time passed and after two years of placement, the mother continued to be evasive and elusive; the father had recently broken an unevenly sustained contact with the boy through the mother's manipulations, with the result that R.F. became very upset. After that incident, the caseworker found the boy less accessible. He became foulmouthed with other children in the cottage and was seen as something of a bully. Gradually, in psychotherapy, it emerged that the boy was an extremely angry youngster who did not trust anyone enough to confide in, felt caught in a situation he did not understand, and could only see flight as a possible resolution. The impression at that time was that he now seemed to be suffering from an unendurable conflict and to be responding to the mother's elusiveness and evasiveness and that she kept him dangling, as she did the men in her life.

Gradually R.F.'s increasing anger was displaced onto other children, and the following year, when R.F. was approaching his fourteenth birthday and after having spent three years at the Pleasantville Cottage School, he was considered generally alert and cooperative but guarded. His productions were coherent and goal directed, and there was no evidence of overt psychosis or other thought disorder. However, he was markedly concrete in his thinking and tended to be somewhat circumstantial. (By this time his mother had remarried and her husband, who was a writer, was employed out of the home.) At that time R.F. was also described as an appealing boy of limited intellect, with poor controls, poor memory, defects in judgment, and an impoverished emotional life. He required special schooling, close supervision, and definite structure.

Consideration was given to a plan for him to return home, but this move was shaky and there was no evidence that the mother would attempt to meet his needs. She probably would have to re-place him as soon as he was in difficulty. It was noted at the time that the boy had few friends but that he was trying to improve his behavior in the sense that he was controlling his anger. He was sloppy and hard on clothes and required many more clothes than the other boys. He retained a number of infantile habit patterns.

Despite the fact that a plan set by the staff called for R.F. to return home, no one felt that this would be a good situation for him. However, because he was unable to relate to any other plan, it seemed necessary to acquiesce to this plan and to have R.F. experience what his home had to offer him. The long-term prospect for this plan was not a good one, however, because he was not only brain damaged but also emotionally impaired so that he would always need a protective and structured situation, possibly throughout his lifetime. Meanwhile, at the recommendation of a psychiatrist, the boy had been placed on medication, but he did not cooperate in this area.

Shortly thereafter, R.F. was returned to his own home, and it was indicated that he would require a regular dosage of Ritalin. At the age of 15, he was referred back to the agency because he was definitely unable to adjust at home and in the community. He had been arrested by the police for allegedly having marijuana in his possession. The case was adjudged at Family Court intake and was closed with the understanding that the family would work with the Post Placement Unit of the Jewish Child Care Association. In the course of this work, the mother showed increasing dissatisfaction with the boy, and finally, when R.F. was 15½, the mother requested placement through a PINS petition. The Family Court probation officer explored possible placements.

There was much indecision with regard to the placement of this boy because of differences of opinion among professional staff members, as well as difficulties with the mother. Finally, it was decided with some reservations to offer placement to R.F. at one of the group residences, and he was so placed at the age of 16. R.F.'s placement in the group residence was short-lived and lasted just through June, July, and August of the year of placement.

At that time it was discovered that R.F. was dealing in marijuana in the neighborhood of the residence and was also involving another youngster from the same residence. At one point he had threatened to throw one of the boys off the roof of the building. A number of boys in the residence seriously complained about R.F.'s behavior, and when confronted with the above facts, R.F. denied everything. His attitude was one of disrespect and outrage. It was the general reaction of staff members at a conference with him that the boy was lying and could not be trusted. During the following week, one of the boys in the residence said that R.F. was cruising the residence neighborhood with a knife. It was suggested that the boy be placed in a drug program but this recommendation proved abortive. He professed considerable hostility toward that program and spoke disparagingly about it in profane language.

After continued difficulties with this boy's relationship to the authority figures in the residence household and his lack of cooperation, the staff finally decided that the boy did not belong there. He was considered to be "potentially a very dangerous young man who needed far tighter structure than could be offered by a group residence." Meanwhile, he had gone to live with another family with whom he had become acquainted when he had been in Pleasantville Cottage School. The family did not want him any longer because he did not respond to discipline. He then asked to be taken back by his mother, who stated that she could not stay with him in the same house and that her husband would not permit him to return. Further efforts to place him in a drug program again proved to be unavailing, in addition to the fact that the stepfather did not approve of the particular placement house recommended. At this point it was decided that the boy should be considered for a residential treatment center and at the age of 16½ he was finally placed at Hawthorne-Cedar Knolls. When this report was first written, R.F. had been at that institution for four months, but no follow-up study on his adjustment there was attempted.

In summary, R.F. had a checkered career with many experiences of separation from the home, with behavior that made it difficult for him to be contained in a family setting as well as a group residence, and with evidence that increasing frustration by the failure of the maternal figure to supply this boy's needs produced increasing anger, rebellion, and pathological behavior. It became clear that R.F.'s unstable behavior was related to a neurological condition, but was further aggravated by his unfavorable experiences in the family setting, the constant rejection by various placements which he precipitated, and the rejection by others because of his persistently disturbing behavior.

Psychiatric Examination

Although at the age of 9, R.F. had been in treatment for some months at a local clinic by a psychologist, he had had a psychiatric evaluation at the Community Guidance Center. The staff had recommended that the mother go into treatment to the exclusion of the boy, but she was dissatisfied with this handling of the problem and with the therapy at the local therapy center. The psychiatrist at the agency spent much more time studying the mother than the boy. He diagnosed the behavior of the boy as "unsocialized aggressive reaction of childhood with immaturity that probably related to a good deal of anxiety." He emphasized that the boy had experienced separations from adult males and had found the female maternal figure unsatisfactory. It was clear that the mother had created great hostility in the boy and that, although he suffered a neurological deficiency and a short attention span, there was evidence that the hostility interfered with his operations in school. He could not conform to required disciplines or chores. His peer relationships were considered transitory because of the hostility he displayed toward them. Those children with whom he did maintain a relationship were also disturbed, acting-out personalities.

When R.F. was 13½ years old, he was seen again by a psychiatrist while he was at the Pleasantville Cottage School. At that time his verbal productions were coherent and goal directed, and there was no evidence of overt psychosis or thought disorder. He was markedly concrete in his thinking and tended to be somewhat circumstantial. This latter quality may have been on a defensive basis. He acknowledged at the time that he had few friends and that he enjoyed many sports. The psychiatrist stated that R.F. had a minimal brain dysfunction with a passive-aggressive, aggressive personality structure. He was immature in his presentation and demonstrated poor social judgment and continued learning difficulties in the school setting. He was considered to be quite unrealistic in many ways and constantly denied many matters that were brought to his attention. When R.F. was past his fourteenth birthday, he was followed up by the same psychiatrist, who decided to effect a clinical trial of Ritalin. After R.F. had taken this medication for a while, it was generally agreed that he was functioning better, showed better self-control, and appeared to be performing better in school. However, he began to rebel against the medication and discontinued it shortly thereafter.

While R.F. was in Post Placement, he was seen again by a psychiatrist because he was in behavioral difficulties. The reason for the session was given as "a psychiatric evaluation of the continued need for Ritalin, which was prescribed because of R.F.'s inability to tolerate sleep-away camp during the past summer." A further reason for the psychiatric session was the boy's arrest for the possession of marijuana. During this interview, R.F. tended to minimize his problems at home and at school by implying that everything was fine in both areas. Questioned about his ambitions and his future life, he was unable to provide any reasonable perspective for himself. He rationalized the discontinuance of his visits to his caseworker with the statement that it required too much time to get to the latter's office.

During this interview R.F. showed considerable resistance to a discussion of his personal life and stated that he had no wish to discuss his personal problems with anyone. He admitted to sporadic intake of his medication but would not discuss this matter further. He displayed anger when the matter of his natural father was raised, and he severely decried his father's desertion of him. While he admitted to a feeling of boredom, he denied any anxiety, nervousness, or tension. Although he had attempted to relate to the psychiatrist as a tough, semidelinquent adolescent, he nevertheless created the impression that behind this mask was a young child who seemed to be crying for help, but who did not seem to know how to help himself. He admitted to lying and to stealing money from coats hanging in closets. He refused to confide any fantasies and was quite angry when asked questions of this kind, saying: "It's none of your business." He resisted the idea of living in a residential setting and insisted that he wished to stay at home.

The psychiatrist's diagnostic impression was that of "a behavior disorder of adolescence with a distinct flavor of organicity. He showed poor judgment, impulsivity, diffuse anger, and was quite concrete." The major recommendation was that the boy needed close supervision.

In general, all the psychiatric examinations indicated that R.F. showed no evidence of psychosis, that R.F. was basically a neurologically damaged person with impulsive behavior, and that this behavior was superimposed with a severe acting-out disturbance based on deprivations in his relationships with parental figures.

Psychological Examinations

R.F. had had many psychological test evaluations, the first of which occurred when he was 7½ years old and the last of which when he was 16½. During all this time, it was generally agreed that R.F. was a boy of dull normal intelligence with considerable disparity in functioning. I.Q.'s generally were in the 80's, although he achieved a verbal I.Q. of 96 at the age of 9½. There was evidence of neurological brain damage, and R.F. was described as an immature youngster with a developmental lag and reading and writing retardation. At the age of 7½, a psychologist recommended that long-term strengthening of ego development would be valuable. Frequent but short-term therapy was also suggested. Even at that time, the psychologist had thought that placement should be seriously considered. Corroboration for minimal brain dysfunction was shown in the psychological examination that was administered when R.F. was nearly 13 years old. At that time he was difficult, irritable, fidgety, and resistive. The negativism was quite pronounced and a considerable reading retardation was revealed. His immaturity was marked by a defensive aggressiveness; he did not trust the examiner and gave the impression of being paranoid. The psychologist made a diagnosis of passive-aggressive personality structure with the emphasis on aggression. R.F. seemed to feel that the testing would be used against him rather than to help him.

The psychologist indicated that the boy was not ready for living in the community and that he would need further psychotherapy and remedial assistance. Because R.F. was not showing improvement in his classes at the Pleasantville Cottage School, the psychologist was asked to determine the cause.

Subsequently, when R.F. was released from the school and returned to his parents under the care of the Post Placement Unit, and was also attending a special school in the tenth grade at the age of 15½, he was referred because he could not adjust at home—he was continually angry, sullen, and defiant. He continued to demonstrate poor judgment and impulsiveness, had frequent fights with the family, and stole from them. It was the general impression during this examination that R.F. was chaotic and haphazard and that this behavior mirrored his inner turmoil. He was extremely distractable, grossly misperceived, overreacted to test demands, showed little insight or reflectiveness, and was highly defensive about how he did on the tests, despite his seeming unconcern. He continued to show dull normal intelligence and school retardation. His self-percept was considered primitive and distorted, and his perception of others was so suffused with feelings of intense pain and anger that his capacity for stable object relations was seen as seriously impaired.

He was considered to be much more vulnerable than he admitted and was very defensive about himself. He projected onto others blame for his underlying feelings of inadequacy and discomfort and adopted a paranoid, defensive attitude. The examiner stated that "self-referential perceptions as well as a posture of hyper-alertness, guardedness and suspiciousness, all contributed to the paranoid picture." Re-placement was recommended, especially in a structured residential treatment center. It was felt that a group residential setting might not be appropriate for him, in view of the level of his pathology and of the potential acting out of his conflicts.

Efforts at Therapeutic Intervention

From the time R.F. was 7½ years old, there had been a number of efforts to provide therapeutic help for him and for the mother. As mentioned earlier, therapy had been tried at the Bureau of Child Guidance, the Community Guidance Center, and the Pleasantville Cottage School. Despite continuous recommendations for therapeutic help and despite efforts attempted during this period, R.F.'s general response had been negative. He related badly, he resisted, and he generally felt that these efforts were unnecessary. On the whole R.F.'s relatedness, not only to therapists but also to most individuals with whom he had contact, was limited to his own personal gain, to self-aggrandizement, and other factors. Occasional relationships with some of his peers did not prove to be long lasting. In spite of all efforts, the acting-out continued and his strong anger, which often antagonized others, continued.

At the time this was written R.F.'s stay at Hawthorne-Cedar Knolls was fraught with the continuation of these patterns. The boy resisted relationships with his social worker, and showed his usual problems in relating, in accepting instructions, and in making an effort to deal with his problems.

Validation Conclusion

There is no doubt that the Separation Anxiety Test accurately predicted how R.F. would react wherever he lived and with whomever he had contact. The weakness of his attachment level was apparent and the hostile acting out dominated the entire picture, as was noted by the high levels of both the hostility reaction and the individuation scores. Evidence of paranoid masochism had been obvious throughout the entire history at home and in the institutions R.F. had attended, and was definitively shown in the Separation Anxiety Test. In fact the efforts made at the Pleasantville Cottage School proved abortive in helping him. Conference notes at that school indicated the degree of frustration felt by his workers, and the pattern continued when he returned to his own home and subsequently to the group residence and the residential treatment center. Throughout the history of this boy it was emphasized that he needed supervision and a controlled environment because of his difficulty in containing his impulsive aggression and the general weakness of his judgment level, all of which had been underscored in the Separation Anxiety Test. The pattern of the test was obviously that of hostile detachment, which is very predictive with regard to the above behavioral patterns. The results of the test proved that the boy would not respond to any insight therapy and would always be a difficult person to deal with. In fact, there was a strong indication in the test that R.F. could be dangerous to other persons. It was generally apparent that medical control of the hostile impulses was necessary and this recommendation might well have been made on the basis of the Separation Anxiety Test alone.

APPENDIX A

Table A-1
Separation Anxiety Test Norms

Table A-2
Chart for Controlled Association Responses

Table A-3
Pattern Summary Chart

TABLE A-1
SEPARATION ANXIETY TEST NORMS
(See Note 1 Below)

Factor	Weak Range of Scores	Adequate Range	Strong Range	Area of Emphasis
Attachment	less than 20%	20-25%	more than 25%	Loneliness
Individuation	less than 15%	16-28%	more than 28%	Adaptation
Hostility	less than 12%	12-14%	more than 15%	Anger
Painful Tension	less than 15%	15-17%	more than 17%	Phobic
Reality Avoidance	less than 10%	10-13%	more than 13%	Withdrawal
Concentration impairment and Sublimation	lower percentage than self-love loss	higher percentage than self-love loss	much higher percent than self-love loss	See Note 2 below.
Self-Love Loss	less than 5%	5- 8%	more than 8%	Intrapunitive
Identity Stress: age 11-12 .... age 13-14	less than 7% less than 10%	7- 9% 10-14%	more than 9% more than 14%	
Attachment-Individuation Balance	less than 28%	28-38%	more than 38%	
Absurd Responses	—	0-3	more than 4	See Note 5
Total Responses	less than 40 (constricted)	40-50—Fair 50-65—Good	more than 65	
Difference Score (Mild—Strong)	less than 18% (see Note 3)	18-22%	more than 22% (see Note 4)	

1. These figures are approximate; figures on individual factors must be considered in relation to one another.
2. This category indicates whether intellectual functioning is disrupted by high sensitivity to separation. It can also be thought of as concern with self-esteem.
3. Examine reactions to cards to determine whether there is excessive reactivity to the mild cards or inadequate reactivity to the strong cards.
4. Examine the cards to determine whether there is inadequate reactivity to mild cards or excessive reactivity to the strong cards.

TABLE A-2
CHART FOR CONTROLLED ASSOCIATION PATTERNS

Picture Number	I	II	III	IV	V	VI	VII	VIII	IX	X	XI	XII	Total	Mild	Strong
Mental Set Response															
Separation Intensity	S	M	M	M	M	S	M	S	M	S	S	S			
Rejection	2	8	15	4*	13	10*	14*	11	15	11*	6	5			
Impaired Concentration	17	11	11	1	6	4	11	15	16	17	16	15			
Phobic Feeling	8	2	9	3	3	3	4	6	2	15	8	11			
Anxiety	9*	16	1	2	11	5	13	12	12*	9	2	10			
Loneliness	5	15	5	16	17	9	6	16	17	16	15	17			
Withdrawal	3	12	8	13	7	12	8	7	3	4	9	14			
Somatic	4	14	2	10	12	11	15	8	14	7	13	7			
Adaptive Reaction	7	7	13	14	14	15	12	4	10	8	11	8			
Anger	11	13	14	6	2	1	5	14	1	1	5	2			
Projection	10	17	3*	17*	8	6	9*	1	6	14	10	6			
Empathy	16	3*	12	9*	1*	13	1	5	13*	10	14	12*			
Evasion	6	1	6	5*	10	14	16	9	4	5	7	4			
Fantasy	14	10	7	15*	5*	17	3	2	9	6	12	9			
Well-Being	1	9	4	8	16	2	17	10*	7	3	4	1			
Sublimation	15*	5	16	7	9	7	10	13	11	12	17*	13			
Intrapunitive	13	4	17	12*	15	16*	2*	3*	8	13	3*	3			
Identity Stress	12	6	10	11	4	8	7	17	5*	2	1	16			
TOTAL															

TABLE A-3
PATTERN SUMMARY CHART

RESPONSE PATTERN	Number of Responses		Total	% of Total Protocol	Area of Emphasis	Comment
	Mild II, III, IV, V, VII, IX	Strong I, VI, VIII, X, XI, XII				
Attachment (Sum of loneliness, and empathy)						
Individuation (Sum of adaptation, well-being, and sublimation)						
Hostility (Sum of anger, projection and intrapunitiveness)						
Painful Tension (Sum of phobic, anxiety, and somatic reactions)						
Reality Avoidance (Sum of withdrawal, evasion, and fantasy)						
Concentration Impairment and sublimation (Self-esteem preoccupation)						
Self-love Loss (Sum of rejection and intrapunitiveness)						
Identity Stress						
Absurd Responses						
Attachment-Individuation Balance						

190

Bibliography

Ainsworth, M.D.S., "Attachment and Dependency; A Comparison," in *Attachment and Dependency*, J.L. Gewirtz (ed.), Winston & Sons, Washington, D.C., 1972, pp. 97-137.

Ainsworth, M.D.S., *Patterns of Attachment*, L. Erlbaum Associates, Hillsdale, N.J., 1979.

Benedek, T., "The Psychosomatic Implicatons of the Primary-Unit Mother-Child," *Amer. J. Orth.*, Vol. XIX, pp. 642-654, 1949.

Blanton, S., *Love or Perish*, Simon and Schuster, New York, 1956.

Bowlby, J., "Grief and Mourning in Infancy and Early Childhood," in *Psychoanalytic Study of the Child*, Vol. XV, pp. 9-52, International Universities Press, New York, 1960.

Bowlby, J., *Loss, Detachment and Defense*, Tavistock Child Development Research Unit, 120 Belsize Lane, London, N.W. 3, 1962.

Bowlby, J., *Attachment and Loss*, Vol. I, Basic Books, New York, 1969.

Bowlby, J., *Separation: Anxiety and Anger*, Basic Books, New York, 1973.

Bowlby, J., "Attachment Theory, Separation Anxiety and Mourning," in D.A. Hamburg and H.K. Brodie (eds.), *American Handbook of Psychiatry*, Vol. VI, New Frontiers in Psychiatry, pp. 292-309, Basic Books, New York, 1974.

Bowlby, J., *Loss, Sadness, and Depression*, Basic Books, New York, 1980.

Bowlby, J., and M. Klagsburn, "Responses to Separation from Parents: A Clinical Test for Young Children," *British J. Proj. Psych.*, Vol. 21, No. 2, December 1976, pp. 7-27.

Brown, G.W., "Meaning, Measurement and Stress of Life Events," in B.S. and B.P. Dolvenrend (eds.), *Stressful Life Events: Their Nature and Effects*, John Wiley & Sons, New York, 1974.

Brown, G.W., H. Tirril, and J.R. Copeland, "Depression and Loss," *British J. Psychia.*, Vol. 130, January 1977, p. 1.

Cannon, W., *Bodily Changes in Pain, Fear, Hunger and Rage*, New York, 1929.

DeFeudis, F.V., "Effects of Environmental Changes on the Incorporation of Carbon Atoms of D-Glucose into Mouse Brain and Other Tissues," *Life Sciences*, Vol. 10 Part II, pp. 1187-1194, Pergamon Press, New York, 1971.

DeFeudis, F.V., "Effects of Differential Housing on the Sub-cellular Distribution of Li (Lithium) in the Brain of Mice," in *Brain Research*, Elsevier Publishing Co., Amsterdam, May, 1972, Vol. 43, pp. 686-689.

DeLozier, P., "An Application of Attachment Theory to the Study of Child Abuse," Doctoral Dissertation, California School of Professional Psychology, Los Angeles, 1979.

Freud, S., *Complete Psychological Works of Sigmund Freud,* Vols. 16 and 18, Hogarth Press, London, 1915 and 1926.

Fries, M.E., and M.S. Woolf, "Some Hypotheses on the Role of the Congenital Activity Type in Personality Development," *Psychoanalytic Study of the Child,* 1953, Vol. 8, pp. 48-62.

Hansburg, H.D., *Adolescent Separation Anxiety: A Method for the Study of Adolescent Separation Problems.* C.C. Thomas, Springfield, Ill., 1972. Reprinted by R. E. Krieger, Pub. Co., Huntington, N.Y. 1980.

Hansburg, H.G., "Adolescent Separation Hostility: A Prelude to Violence," in *Abstract Guide of XXth International Congress of Psychology,* Tokyo, 1972, p. 599.

Hansburg, H.G., "Separation Problems of Displaced Children," in R. Parker (ed.), *The Emotional Stress of War, Violence and Peace,* Stanwix House, Pittsburgh, 1972, pp. 241-262.

Hansburg, H.G., "Some Generalizations with Regard to Studies of Families with the Separation Anxiety Test" (unpublished study), 1975.

Hansburg, H.G., "The Use of the Separation Anxiety Test in the Detection of Self-Destructive Tendencies in Early Adolescence," in D.V. Siva Sankar (ed.), *Mental Health in Children,* Vol. III, P.J.D. Publications, Westbury, N.Y., 1976, pp. 161-199.

Hansburg, H.G., *Separation Disorders of the Elderly,* (in press).

Harlow, H., "Nature of Love, Simplified," *Amer. Psychologist,* Vol. 25, February 1970, pp. 161-168.

Kagan, J., *The Growth of the Child,* W.W. Norton & Co., New York, 1978.

Kagan, J., R.B. Kersley, and P.R. Zelazo, *Infancy, Its Place in Human Development,* Harvard University Press, Cambridge, Mass., 1978.

Klein, M., *Contributions to Psychoanalysis,* 1921-1945, Hogarth Press, London, 1948.

Konner, M.J., quoted by J. Greenberg in *Science News Letter,* Vol. 112, July 30, 1977, "The Brain and Emotions," pp. 74-75.

Levy, L.H., *Psychological Interpretation,* Holt, Rhinehart and Winston, New York, 1963, p. 157.

Mahler, M., *On Human Symbiosis and the Vicissitudes of Individuation,* Vol. 1, International University Press, New York, 1968.

Masterson, J.F., *Treatment of the Borderline Adolescent,* John Wiley & Sons, New York, 1972.

McKinney, W., H. Harlow, and S.J. Suomi, "Depression in Primates," *Amer. J. Psychia.,* Vol. 27, No. 10, 1971, pp. 49-56.

McKinney, W. *et al.,* "Effects of Reserpine on the Social Behavior of Rhesus Monkeys," *Diseases of the Nervous System,* Vol. 32, No. 11, November, 1971.

McKinney, W. *et al.,* "Studies in Depression," *Psychology Today,* May 1971, p. 63.

McKinney, W. *et al.,* "Chlorpromazine Treatment of Disturbed Monkeys," *Archives of General Psychiatry,* Vol. 29, 1973.

Niederland, W., *Selected Papers* in H. Krystal (ed.), *Massive Psychic Trauma,* International University Press, New York, 1968.

Peterfreund, E., "Information, Systems and Psychoanalysis," *Psychological Issues,* Vol. VII, Monograph 25/26, International University Press, New York, 1971.

Rosenzweig, S., *Psychodiagnosis,* Grune & Stratton, Inc., New York, 1949.

Schaffer, R., *Aspects of Internalization,* International University Press, New York, 1968.

Scott, J.P. and E.C. Senay, *Separation and Depression,* Pub. No. 94, A.A.A.S., Washington, D.C., 1973.

Seligman, M., "Helplessness," in W.H. Freeman (ed.), *On Depression, Development and Death,* San Francisco, 1975.

Smith, M.B., "Perspectives on Selfhood," *Amer. Psychologist,* Vol. 33, No. 12, pp. 1053-1063, December 1978.

Suomi, S.J., "Social Development of Rhesus Monkeys Reared in an Enriched Laboratory Environment," *Abstract Guide of XXth International Congress of Psychology,* Tokyo, 1972.

Thomas, A., S. Chess, and H.G. Birch, *Temperament and Behavior Disorders in Children,* New York University Press, 1968.

White, R., *Ego and Reality in Psychoanalytic Theory,* International University Press, New York, 1963.

Winnicott, D.W., *Collected Papers,* Tavistock, London, 1958.

Witkin, H.A. *et al., Psychological Differentiation,* John Wiley & Sons, New York, 1962.

Wolfenstein, M., "Loss, Rage and Repetition," *Psychoanalytic Study of the Child,* Vol. 24, International University Press, New York, 1969, pp. 432-460.

INDEX

Masochism. *see* Self-destructive
behavior
Masterson, 45
Maturation pocess, 39
Memory stores
and anxious attachment, 14
episodic, 11
semantic, 12
Mental Set Questions, 33

Narcissism, 10
Narcissistic destruction, 35
Neurosis, 1
Niederland, 11
Norms for Separation Anxiety Test,
188

Pattern frequencies. *see* Interpretation
of pattern frequencies.
Pattern Summary Chart, 190
Peterfreund, 8
Phobic responses, 34, 49
Physiological systems
deactivation of, 20
similarity to psychological system,
20
Projection responses, 32, 37
Projective tests, 30
Protocols. *see* Interpretation of
protocols with case materials.
Proximity-seeking, 4
Psychodiagnosis, 28
Psychological systems
attachment, 3-4
deactivation of, 8, 9
defensive, 8-9
definition of, 2-3
fear-anxiety-pain, 5-6
and homeostasis, 9
hostility, 7-8
individuation, 4-5
and interpretation of item frequency,
40
and memory stores, 11-12
and separation disorders, 12
and separation experiences, 11
sexual, 11
similarity to physiological systems, 2

Reality avoidance, 9, 52
Reality avoidance response patterns, 25

Rejection responses, 36, 37, 43, 55
Repression, 8
Response frequency. *see* Interpretation of response frequency on
Separation Anxiety Test.
Rosenzweig, 28

Sadomasochistic interaction, 18
Schaffer, 21
Scott, 25
Self-destructive behavior
and affect reactions, 49
and anxious attachment, 16, 17
and depressive syndrome, 24, 25
and intrapunitive response, 37
masochism, 11, 16
and self-love loss, 54, 55, 56
suicide, 11, 16
Self-esteem response patterns, 57-59
Self-esteem system, 10, 11
Self-evaluative system
and anxious attachment, 15
and detachment, 21
and homeostasis, 9
and identity stress response, 39
in infancy, 9
patterns of, 54-61
and separation experiences, 11
sub-systems of, 10-11
Self-love, definition of, 10
Self-love loss response pattern
and depressive syndrome, 24, 25
and excessive self-sufficiency, 24
interpretation of, 54-57
Self-love system
definition of, 10, 11
loss of in anxious attachment, 15
Self-reliance system. *see* Individuation
system.
Self-sufficiency
excessive, 23-24
and individuation system, 5
Seligman, 25
Senary, 25
Separation
See also Separation disorders.
and affect blunting, 48
anxiety (as a term), 6
and anxious attachment, 13-17
and attachment patterns, 43
and defensive beliefs, 9